Table of Contents.

Introduction.	6
Chapter 1. Schumpeter's Gales of Creative Destruction.	27
Chapter 2. Declining Marginal Costs of Production in the New World Order Macrotechnology.	44
Chapter 3. The Failure of New World Order Globalism in Promoting National Economic Growth and Shared Prosperity.	56
Chapter 4. Updating Schumpeter's Entrepreneurial Economic Growth Model As the Economic Alternative to the Corporate New World Order.	72
Chapter 5. Adding Christensen's Analysis of Radical Disruptive Innovation to Schumpeter's Entrepreneurial Economic Growth Model.	78
Chapter 6. Connecting Schumpeter's Entrepreneurial Innovation to Christensen's Economic Growth Tool of Blockchain Innovation.	85
Chapter 7. The Blockchain Innovation Economic Growth Model of New Venture Creation.	89
Chapter 8. Exploiting the Vulnerability of New World Order Crony Corporatism.	98
Bibliography.	126

Schedule of Diagrams and Exhibits.

Diagram 1. Depiction of Schumpeter's Concept of the Economy Either Growing or Dying.   8

Diagram 2. Economy Breaking Away From Equilibirum to a Nash Equilibrium.   36

Diagram 3. Selected U.S. China Business Council Member Companies, Names Starting With letter A.   61

Diagram 4. Selected Member CEOs and Companies of the Business Roundtable Whose Company Name Begins With the Letter A Who Are Also Member Companies of the USCBC.   62

Diagram 5. Chronological Sequence of Events of a Radical Innovation Leading to A Potential Market Disruption.   83

Diagram 6. Regional Blockchain New Technology Venture Creation Model.   91

Diagram 7. New World Order Assumptions and Propositions.   99

Updating Schumpeter's Gales of Creative Destruction:

Exploiting the Vulnerability of New World Order Corporate Globalism With Regional Blockchain Entrepreneurial Economic Growth.

Laurie Thomas Vass

Copyright © 2022 The Great American Business & Economics Press. GABBYPress.

First edition. All rights reserved under Title 17, U.S. Code, International and Pan-American copyright Conventions.

No part of this work may be reproduced or transmitted in any form or by any means, electronic or mechanical, including photocopying, scanning, recording or duplication by any information storage or retrieval system without prior written permission from the author(s) and publisher(s), except for the inclusion of brief quotations with attribution in a review or report. Requests for reproductions or related information should be addressed to the author c/o Great American Business & Economics Press, 620 Kingfisher Lane SW, Sunset Beach, N. C. 28468.
Printed in the United States of America. June 2022.

Updating Schumpeter's Gales of Creative Destruction: Exploiting the Vulnerability of New World Order Corporate Globalism With Regional Blockchain Entrepreneurial Economic Growth.

Laurie Thomas Vass. The Citizens Liberty Party

Introduction.

In Capitalism, Socialism and Democracy, Joseph Schumpeter described capitalism as an evolutionary economic growth theory. [J. A. Schumpeter, Capitalism, Socialism and Democracy, George Allen & Unwin, 1942.].

If there is a dynamic force within the free market system that can be explained by the natural laws of supply and demand, then Schumpeter explained that the free market economy is either growing or it is dying.

Schumpeter states,

"The essential point to grasp is that in dealing with capitalism we are dealing with an evolutionary process. ... Capitalism, then, is by nature a form or method of economic change and not only never is but never can be stationary...The funndamental impulse that sets and keeps the capitalist engine in motion comes from the new consumers' goods, the new methods of production or transportation, the new markets, the new forms of industrial organization that capitalist enterprise creates. ... This process of Creative Destruction is the essential fact about capitalism.

It is what capitalism consists in and what every capitalist concern has got to live in."

The creative destructive force is caused by entrepreneurial innovation in new products and new technology. [J. A. Schumpeter, The Theory of Economic Development. Harvard University Press. First published in German, 1911.].

From any point of equilibrium, according to Schumpeter, the economy could trace out an upward path of economic growth, to a new equilibrium, or, it could trace out a downward path of economic decline.

We offer a depiction of Schumpeter's economic evolutionary theory in Diagram 1.

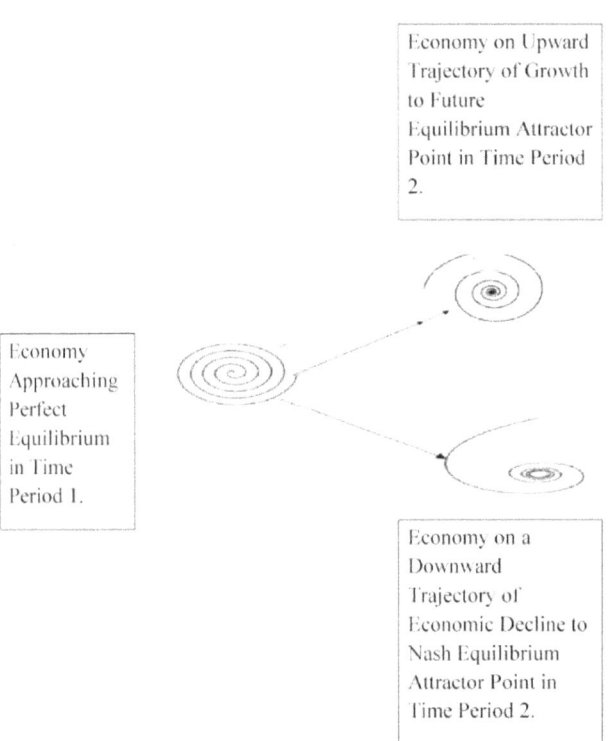

Diagram 1. Depiction of Schumpeter's Concept of the Economy Either Growing or Dying.

Schumpeter's concept of economic evolution was in contrast to the prevailing wisdom of the time that the economy would return to the prior equilibrium after a perturbation knocked the economy out of equilibrium,

Schumpeter also broke with traditional macro economic theory by suggesting that the source of capital for investment for new manufacturing ventures was from capital gain exit events from prior ventures.

In Schumpeter's analysis of the source of investment capital, it could either be a loan from a commercial bank, or it could be the capital gain profit from an earlier successful venture.

The source of capital was rarely from the personal savings of the entrepreneur.

Schumpeter states,

"However great the role of self-financing may be in the course of the development of an enterprise, the original nucleus of means [capital] has been but rarely acquired by the entrepreneur's own saving activity which in fact is one of the reasons, and a significant one, for distinguishing the entrepreneur as sharply as I think he should be distinguished from the capitalist."

His break with the neo classical economic tradition was that the supply of capital for new investment was not derived from price-based retail and wholesale exchanges in either the intermediate demand sphere of production, or in the finished goods, final demand market.

As Schumpeter stated,

"By far, the greater part of it [capital] does not come from thrift in the strict sense, that is from abstaining from the consumption of part of one's regular income, but it consists of funds which are themselves the result of successful innovation, and in which we shall see later recognize entrepreneurial profit."

Schumpeter believed that, if and when, the capitalist system was growing, the benefits of the economic growth would be widely distributed throughout the society.

He wrote,

"The capitalist process, not by coincidence but by virtue of its mechanism, progressively raises the standard of life of the masses." [Capitalism, Socialism, and Democracy.].

Towards the end of his life, Schumpeter became pessimistic about the trends that he saw in the U. S. economy towards monopoly capitalism, which would act as a barrier to further technological innovation, and consequently lead to declining rates of economic growth.

In the absence of technological innovation, the economy would stop growing, leading to Schumpeter's analysis that the next logical step of the economy was to national socialism, as citizens turned against the political-economic structure of monopoly capitalism.

Schumpeter explained that the relationship between entrepreneurship and national economic growth was a result of technology innovation caused by capital investments in new technology ventures.

Schumpeter emphasized that the process of technological innovation brought about by capital investments in new entrepreneurial ventures made existing products and older manufacturing processes obsolete [extinct].

He used the term economic evolution to describe this process of technological innovation, and his use of the term "evolution" was probably 100 years ahead of its time.

He wrote during a period of time when the basic unit of economic analysis for macro economic growth and international trade was the sovereign nation state.

For example, both David Ricardo's theory of comparative advantage, and the Heckscher–Ohlin theory of international trade begin with an initial assumption that the units of analysis are one national economy compared to a second national economy.

Their theories of the benefits of international trade were based upon the diverse national factor endowments between nations. Their theories were designed to explain and predict how different factor endowments would lead to increased national social welfare, in both national economies, as a result of international trade.

In his Nobel Laureate speech, Simon Kuznets also places the economic unit of analysis for macro economics into the nation-state framework. [Modern Economic Growth: Findings and Reflections, 1971.].

Kuznets stated,

"A country's economic growth may be defined as a long-term rise in capacity to supply increasingly diverse economic goods to its population, this growing capacity based on advancing technology and the institutional and ideological adjustments that it (technological advancement) demands… Mass application of technological innovations, which constitutes much of the distinctive substance of modern economic growth, is closely connected with the further progress of science, in its turn the basis for additional advance in technology."

Writing more recently, Edmund Phelps links the prosperity generated by technological innovation to a nation's economic progress. [Edmund S. Phelps, Refounding Capitalism, Capitalism and Society, 2009, Reprinted in SSRN.].

Phelps writes,

"Over the past decade I have maintained *that countries* would still benefit from the innovative activity of original thinkers, visionary entrepreneurs, canny investors, pioneering managers and devoted employees that, starting in the 19th century and in *some countries* ending in the 20th, drew an ever widening share of people in an ever-growing number of nations into engaging jobs, exciting explorations and remarkable commercial advances of innovation: the conception of novel commercial ideas, the selection by financiers of some of these ideas for development, the realization by entrepreneurs of the envisioned products or methods, and the adoption or rejection by managers or consumers of some of the new products reaching the market." [emphasis added].

Like Schumpeter's analysis of the merits of the capitalist system, Phelps also raised the question of the benefits of free markets over the operation of centralized, collectivist economies.

Kuznets concludes his Nobel Laureate address about capitalism with this statement,

"For many, capitalism's main merits are the wealth accumulation it fosters and the "individual freedom" it helps to protect… Could it be that the value of a well-functioning capitalism in providing participants with opportunities to act on their own knowledge, intuition and judgment, and in providing opportunities to be engaged and to flourish serves to justify that capitalism?"

We argue that it is not the virtues of corporate monopoly capitalism that serves as the justification of capitalism.

Rather, we point to Schumpeter's advocacy of entrepreneurial capitalism, cited above by Kuznets, as the logical justification of the U. S. economic system.

Our term for that form of capitalism is "entrepreneurial capitalism," a description first coined by William Baumol, et al., in 2007.

Baumol writes

"The U.S. economy has achieved a remarkable transformation over the last several decades from an economy characterized by large, bureaucratic firms into one increasingly powered by entrepreneurial innovation. The challenge ahead therefore is to cement and strengthen the entrepreneurial form of capitalism… the continuing emergence and growth of innovative companies -- or what we label "entrepreneurial capitalism" stands in stark contrast to the dominance of large firms and unions in the United States in the decades immediately after the end of World War II, and also to the continuing dominance of large firms in Western Europe and Japan." [William J. Baumol, Robert E. Litan, Carl J Schramm, Sustaining Entrepreneurial Capitalism, Capitalism and Society, 2007. Reprinted SSRN. 2013.].

While we agree with Baumol on the promotion of an entrepreneurial capitalist economy, we disagree with Baumol about the factual history of the emergence of the entrepreneurial capitalist society in the United States.

Our interpretation of history is that after the collapse of the Berlin Wall, in 1989, a new theory of global trade began to emerge that featured an open, borderless global market, where large corporations traded goods in a seamless international market.

This new form of global trade subordinated the role of national governments, and replaced the unit of economic analysis from nation states to an analysis of the economics of a global stateless market dominated by trade among large corporations.

In this new version of global corporatism, large corporations collaborate with two other interest groups, labor unions, and agencies of the deep-state institutional apparatus, to set the rules of international trade and negotiate over the distribution of income among social classes.

For example, in 2019, The Business Roundtable adopted a new mission statement calling for more collaboration and negotiation over the distribution of benefits from corporations.

The new Business Roundtable mission describes the new form of global capitalism as "stakeholder capitalism."

In the new global stakeholder economy, the purposes of the large corporations to "create value for customers, invest in employee's [welfare], foster [multicultural] diversity and inclusion, deal fairly and ethically with suppliers, support the communities where the corporation is located [globalism], and protect the environment."

Our term for this new version of capitalism is crony global corporatism.

This shift in the unit of economic analysis from nation states to corporations has been described as a new world order, which does not require the existence of nation state governments in order to function in the global market.

In the U.S., a version of crony corporate capitalism replaced the former constitutional representative republic with the operation of a Leviathan that functions entirely independent of the consent of the governed.

The common name for the modern Leviathan is the "Deep State."

This transition to the global corporatism, after 1989, has been called the "great reset," which implies a reset from sovereign nation states to a new world order of global corporate fascism, where global corporations direct non-governmental organizations [NGOs], to perform functions previously performed by the governments of nations.

In other words, a "one-world-government," that functions on a rule-based framework, not a citizen democratic framework, is required by corporations to manage trade relationships among global corporations.

The emphasis of economic analysis in the new world order shifts, from examining the welfare differences among nations, caused by economic growth, to the analysis of how global corporations can meet concerns of global fairness and global environmental issues brought to their attention by NGO constituencies [stakeholders].

In other words, under new world order globalism, the macro general equilibrium economic analysis changes from the dynamics of national economic welfare to the maintenance of a negotiated global technological status quo, in a zero-sum corporate globalism.

The data for global analysis shifts from improvements of national social welfare to the analysis of how the profits of large corporations are distributed to meet social issues, as if profits of global corporations are surrogate indicators of improvements in global social welfare.

The initial, unstated, unverified assumption of the new corporate world order, after 1989, is that global social welfare would be better under the new world order than it would be under the national sovereignty model of economic growth because all nations, including China, would transition to a middle class society as a consequence of global trade.

The public relations ploy of the corporations, after 1989, was that China was just like the U. S. and would transition from a communist society to a pluralist democracy as a result of admitting China into the World Trade Organization.

In the 2018 annual report to Congress, the U.S. Trade Representative's Office stated,

"It seems clear that the United States erred in supporting China's entry into the WTO on terms that have proven to be ineffective in securing China's embrace of an open, market-oriented trade regime,"

Rather than move in the direction of open competitive markets, Xi entrenched communist control over the economy in his bid for world domination.

In 2012, the year before Xi's elevation to permanent power, more than half of Chinese bank loans went to private firms; by 2015, that fell to 19 percent. Loans to state-ruling owned enterprises, by comparison, doubled to 69 percent.

Newt Gingrich is quoted in October, 2019, explaining this American misconception about trade with China,

"For many decades, Americans thought communist-ruled China would evolve into a free China. Under Xi, China is developing an ultra-high-tech police state, wherein powerful cameras and facial recognition artificial intelligence are being utilized to control the Chinese people in ways we had previously only imagined in science fiction. We thought that the trade agreements would lead to open systems similar to our own. We were completely wrong." [The Hill, October 25, 2019.].

Robert Lighthizer, a U. S. Trade representative under President Trump, made the same point in 2019, when he stated,

"The United States made the mistake of treating China as if it was another democracy. The world trading system created by the General Agreement on Tariffs and Trade in 1947 excluded countries like China for good reason, the earlier trade agreements excluded communist countries because they thought such countries would sabotage GATT."

The rhetoric and propaganda of proponents of the new world order is that the global middle class is growing faster, and therefore, global social welfare is improving more than it would under the national sovereignty economic model.

The logic about the welfare benefits of the new world order is flawed because it assumes, without verification, that the global middle class is increasing in size, and that the presumed growth of the middle class is, ipso facto, proof of the benefits of globalism.

The improvement in global social welfare can never be empirically tested or verified, under traditional macro general equilibrium theory, because global trade's unit of analysis is one global economy, not a comparative analysis of social welfare improvements of the middle class, in independent nation states.

In his article, "Critical Theory," the socialist thinker, James Bohman, describes that the new globalism means that citizen democracy must be replaced by autocratic corporate elite decision-making,

"Existing forms of democracy within the nation-state must be transformed and that institutions ought to be established that solve problems that transcend national boundaries. Globalization is thus taken as a constraint on democracy as it is realized in existing liberal representative systems." [James Bohman, Critical Theory, Republicanism, and the Priority of Injustice: Transnational Republicanism as a Nonideal Theory," Journal of Social Philosophy, 2012.].

The corporate logic of admitting China into the World Trade Organization [WTO], was summarized, in 2000, by Michael Bonsignore, CEO of Honeywell, in his testimony to Congress, in favor of Normal Trade Relations, with China.

Bonsignore, was the lead corporate lobbyist for the Business Roundtable, and he stated that Honeywell was doing over half a billion dollars, annually, in supply chain trade with China.

Bonsignore stated,

"On virtually every Boeing aircraft shipped to China, Honeywell's avionics, auxillary power units, wheels, and brakes are on board. We ship industrial instruments and systems to help modernize a wide range of Chinese industries, from pulp and paper to petrochemicals."

After China was admitted to the WTO, the Chinese government used Honeywell's technology to create nuclear missile guidance systems that can land a nuclear bomb within 80 yards of its intended target.

The new world order of the global corporatism features a global macrotechnology that is the same for all corporations around the globe. Internet communication technology [ICT], allows every corporation to see, and implement, a technology innovation at the same time as any other corporation.

Hyman Minsky has called global corporatism "managed corporate capitalism," because both the pace and direction of technological innovation and the market price of goods must be managed, under a collaborative, not a price-competitive model of the economy. [Hyman Minsky "Schumpeter: Finance and Evolution," in Arnold Heertje and Mark Perlman [Eds], Evolving Technology and Market Structure: Studies in Schumpeterian Economics, University of Michigan Press, 1990.].

Under the conditions of global managed capitalism, the big pension funds, mutual funds, trust funds, otherwise known as institutional money, require predictable cash flows in the near term to support the stock prices and the bond prices in their heavy levels of indebtedness on liability structures, such as mortgage backed securities, which they have securitized.

Prices of goods must be managed by the corporations to provide stable, predictable flows of revenues to provide consistent flows of interest payments to the institutional investment banks.

Corporate control over the global macrotechnology is the weak link, and vulnerable point of attack, for updating Schumpeter's gales of creative destruction of the new world order.

Global corporations require controlled technological innovation, and global crony capitalism, in order to direct the benefits of innovation to themselves, and their crony stakeholders.

The vulnerability of the new world order is that Schumpeter's updated entrepreneurial blockchain innovation is beyond the control of global corporations.

If global corporations cannot control the pace of technological innovation, they would lose control over managing and setting prices in the collaborative global economic model.

Consequently, if they lose control over the prices of products, they would lose control over the distribution of income that benefits themselves and their crony government agents.

We update Schumpeter's original analysis, by placing his concept of the gales of creative destruction within the modern framework of Clayton Christensen's concept of blockchain innovation.

The income and wealth benefits of blockchain entrepreneurial economic growth are widely distributed, and geographically decentralized, throughout the national society.

In blockchain entrepreneurial innovation, open flows of tacit knowledge are enhanced by the ability of the computer algorithm to identify the participants in the knowledge chain who are contributing shared tacit knowledge.

In the global macrotechnology, the formerly open flows of tacit knowledge are internalized within the legal organizational entities of large corporations in order to avoid technological knowledge from slipping off the plate of a corporation, [spillover], and potentially falling onto the plate of a new venture not controlled by the corporations.

Clayton Christensen has called this inadvertent release of technological knowledge a "disruptive technological innovation."

What Christensen means is that the inadvertent release of technological knowledge potentially disrupts the revenue flows of large corporations in the managed global economy.

Christensen's term for non-disruptive innovation is "sustaining innovation," because it is controlled within the corporate legal structure.

Sustaining innovation within the corporation is primarily created by "codified" knowledge, which means the knowledge is in the form of proprietary written text, which can only be shared with selected interested parties, outside the corporate structure.

Christensen writes from the perspective of what improves the welfare of the corporation, not in terms of how economic growth benefits the social welfare of citizens in nation-states.

However, Christensen's classification of the types of innovation that affect the welfare of global corporations provides the strategy for exploiting the weakness of the new world order of corporate fascism.

The weakness of global corporatism is that codified technological innovation does not create global economic growth.

Kuznets makes a distinction in the classification of technological innovations, some of which may provide future economic welfare benefits.

Kuznets states,

"A technological innovation, particularly one based on a recent major invention, represents a venture into the partly unknown… Those [innovations] of most interest here are the surprises, the unexpected results, which may be positive or negative. An invention or innovation may prove far more productive, and induce a far wider mass application and many more cumulative improvements than were dreamed of by the inventor and the pioneer group of entrepreneurs."

Chistensen calls "the unexpected results," of innovation a "radical" innovation, in contrast to the sustaining innovation, that is controlled by the corporations.

According to Christensen, radical innovation creates new future markets, which causes economic growth. Radical innovation, caused by tacit knowledge, creates future economic growth.

Codified knowledge technological innovation, controlled by global corporations, does not cause future economic growth because it does not create new future markets.

To return to Schumpeter's analysis of the capitalist system, it is either growing or it is dying. And, under controlled corporate technological innovation, the economy is on a path of economic decline.

In the absence of radical innovation, an economy grows slowly, or slips into a lower Nash equilibrium. The vulnerability of the new world order is the emergence of uncontrolled radical innovation, which causes macro economic growth.

In contrast to Baumol's prediction of the emergence of entrepreneurial capitalism, we explain that the main consequence of the global corporate control over technological innovation, is that the American economy has suffered a lower rate of technological innovation, and consequently reduced rates of economic growth, after China was admitted to the World Trade Organization, in 2001.

In the absence of real economic growth, after 2001, the U. S. economy has reverted to a permanent boom-bust-bubble economy, caused by monetary and currency manipulation, coordinated by the Fed and global central banks, not real economic growth caused by private business capital investment in new technological ventures..

The mirage of economic growth of global central bank monetary manipulation, replaced the real economic growth that was formerly caused by capital investment in small technology ventures, which primarily took place in 300 of the largest U. S. metro regions.

Under corporate globalism, we argue that the benefits of economic growth that result from sustaining technological innovation are internalized and captured by large corporations.

We explain that under Schumpeter's entrepreneurial economic growth model, national interindustry relationships [supply chains] are the communication pathways of diffusing tacit technical knowledge.

In contrast to entrepreneurial capitalism, the new world order global macrotechnology features corporate supply chains tightly controlled and centralized by large corporations in very few locations, such as the large metro regions of China.

Control over the interindustry supply chains allows the corporations to control the spread of potentially disruptive radical technological knowledge.

Based upon an analysis of the components of U. S. GDP, after the economic collapse of 2008, about 80% of all GDP was related to six service industrial sectors, which employ about 70% of the U. S. workforce, [gig economy].

About 20% of U. S. GDP is related to the industrial sectors engaged in global trade, in the global corporate macrotechnology.

We estimate that the new world order economic model benefits about 20% of the U. S. population, who get richer and richer from the operation of the global corporate model.

We argue that the ultimate economic consequence of new world corporatism is world-wide economic decline because there is insufficient technological innovation to allow the global economy to break free of the trend to a global Nash equilibrium.

In the absence of open, tacit, technological innovation, the rate of private domestic capital investment in new entrepreneurial ventures will continue to decline, causing the economic growth rates in the U. S. national economy to decline.

As the U. S. economic growth rates continue to decline, the social welfare consequences for the 80% of the U. S. population that does not benefit from global trade, will also continue to decline.

The corporate new world order is a failure because the system functions to deliberately lower the rate of economic growth that could be achieved under a fair competitive price system, and limits distribution of the welfare benefits of economic growth to a self-selected social class of elites.

The managed crony capitalist corporate global system allows the large corporations to gain political control over the pace of technological innovation by replacing citizen participatory democracy, in each nation, with an autocratic NGO one-world-government.

We argue that the solution to the new world order of global corporate fascism is to blow the global corporate economy away with radical technological innovation of Updating Schumpeter's gales of creative destruction with blockchain entrepreneurial capitalist economic growth represents a new economic model that the new world order is unable to control.

Chapter 1. Schumpeter's Gales of Creative Destruction.

In his early writings, Joseph Schumpeter described the internal dynamic forces of the free market as akin to the "gales of creative destruction."

In The Theory of Economic Development, Schumpeter begins with a review of the basic economic equilibrium concepts that describe the recurring economic processes of a commercially organized state in which private property, division of labor, and free competition prevail.

These economic forces constitute what Schumpeter calls "the circular flow of economic life," such as consumption, factors and means of production, labor, value, prices, cost, exchange, money as a circulating medium, and exchange value of money.

Schumpeter argued that the equilibrium of a "circular flow" concept of economic growth did not guarantee that the economy would return to the prior equilibrium, after an economic disturbance knocked the economy out of equilibrium.

Rather, Schumpeter argued that the capitalist economy was dynamic and changed its form and shape as a result of technical innovations in the production process, and the introduction of new products.

According to Schumpeter, the "new thing," created by the entrepreneur is based upon the entrepreneur's application of technology, and comes into the market alongside of the "old thing."

The major model of dynamic of economic evolution for Schumpeter was the Darwinian competition among species, and the elimination of the weaker species by the stronger species.

He stated,

"The new enterprises either completely eliminate old businesses or else force them to restrict their operations…The [new] demand...causes a rise in the prices of productive services. From this [rise in prices] ensues the withdrawal of goods from their previous use...the newly created purchasing power [new incomes] is squeezed out at the cost of previously existing purchasing power..."

According to Schumpeter, in the later stages of monopoly capitalism, the concentrated ownership of corporations would breed a political hostility towards capitalism by the working and middle classes, who were no longer benefitting from economic growth.

In contrast to monopoly capitalism, Schumpeter argued that a large number of entrepreneurs and a widespread ownership of firms would create a political climate that is favorable towards the creation of an entrepreneurial capitalist system.

Magnus Henrekson and Ulf Jakobsson offered six logical propositions related to Schumpeter's analysis of monopoly capitalism, as it is applied to the historical context of the Swedish economy's attempt to implement a socialist economy. [Magnus Henrekson, Ulf Jakobsson, Where Schumpeter was Nearly Right - The Swedish Model and

Capitalism, Socialism and Democracy, Journal of Evolutionary Economics, 2001. Reprinted in SSRN. 2007.].

Their six propositions are listed below:

1. Under monopoly capitalism, the bulk of innovations will be made in large corporations.
2. Large corporations will be increasingly predominant in the economy.
3. New and smaller firms will play a declining role in the economy.
4. The concentration of ownership will grow over time.
5. The general public, not least the intellectuals, will grow increasingly hostile towards capitalism. Wages would be set in wage negotiations between labor unions and corporate management, as per the globalist negotiation model, Dividends would be related to the level of interest rates in capital markets, and all excess profits would remain within the companies.
6. Socialism, as in the historical case of Sweden, will eventually replace capitalism.

Henrekson and Jacobsson explain,

"The evolution of the Swedish economy closely followed Schumpeter's predictions until about 1980: Large firms became increasingly predominant in production and innovative activity, ownership of firms became more and more concentrated, individual entrepreneurship waned in importance, the general public grew increasingly hostile towards capitalism, and by the late 1970s explicit proposals for a gradual transfer of ownership of firms from private hands [to worker-owned enterprises] were launched."

They concluded that the Marxian analysis of the ability of monopoly capitalism to adapt to threats by co-opting the opposition was true in Sweden, which explained why the transition to socialism failed, after 1980.

They write,

"Our view, supported by the evidence reviewed here, is that entrepreneurship, ownership and risk-bearing cannot be fully separated. Hence, policies and institutions that channel assets away from individual control will curtail the deployment of entrepreneurial talent and drive. The system was thus favoring investments and accumulation of capital in the corporate sector at the same time as it was unfavorable towards private wealth creation."

We argue that the new collaborative global corporatism, in Sweden, is another version of the crony capitalist system co-opting the socialist threat by providing their enemies with a seat at the negotiating table, in order to negotiate income distribution between social class special interest groups.

In the historical example of Sweden, the concentration of control and ownership of large corporations increased, after 1980, while the national GDP stagnated as a consequence of the political allegiance to the status quo of corporate global crony collaboration.

In other words, to apply Schumpeter's analysis of equilibrium to Sweden's history, the economic pie stopped growing, after 1980, and the collaboration between labor unions and corporate management, after 1980, was over an increasingly small amount of national income.

At that moment in time, in Schumpeter's analysis of the circular flow of production and consumption, there is, according to Yasar,

'A stationary situation of equilibrium and perfect competition similar to a so-called Walrasian state of equilibrium." [Ayse Gizem Yasar, Re-examining Schumpeter's Legacy: Creative Destruction as Competition, Innovation and Capitalism,SSRN 2021.].

Yazar describes how global corporations are able to co-opt their enemies, in a static, non-growing economy.

He writes,

"When there is no perfect competition and when each industrial field is controlled by a few big concerns, these [corporations] can in various ways fight the threatening attack on their capital structure and try to avoid losses on their capital accounts; that is to say, they can and will fight progress [socialism] itself."

In Schumpeter's entrepreneurial capitalism, the new entrepreneurial ventures are not subsidiaries or divisions of existing production units.

In Schumpeter, the new enterprise,

"...does not grow out of the old, but appears alongside of it, and eliminates it [the old enterprise] competitively, so as to change all the conditions that a special process of adaptation becomes necessary."

If the capital gain profits from the exit events from earlier investments in new ventures are subsequently re-invested in the second time period, according to Schumpeter, the effect of the investment in time period two is to create new income and wealth in time period three.

He described a dynamic economic growth sequence of new ventures replacing old ventures and creating new flows of income in the future.

Schumpeter states,

"It is not essential that the new combinations [ventures] should be carried out by the same people who control the production or commercial process [in the older firms]...new combinations mean the competitive elimination of the old...It [the investment process] in new firms explains on the one hand the process by which individuals and families rise and fall economically and socially...In a non-exchange economy, for example, a socialist one...the social consequences [of the investment process] would be wholly absent."

His insight into the maintenance of the social class status quo of the existing ruling class in socialist societies applies equally well to the current allegiance to the status quo distribution of income in the new world order corporatist economy.

If large corporations, for example, in Sweden, can control the direction of technological change, then upward occupational mobility of the working and middle classes can be controlled.

Schumpeter explained that from the perspective of classical economics, which was based upon conflict between two social classes, the political and financial allegiance of the ruling class to the status quo diminished the ability of the economy to reproduce itself.

The investment process in new firms created new income in the future, which Schumpeter called "purchasing power."

The new purchasing power in time period three was a potential capital fund for more capital investments, and, if capital happened to be invested in a new round of new ventures, then the dynamic economic growth pattern may continue, contingent on a continued rate of capital investment in new ventures.

Schumpeter explained that this capital re-investment process was how economy reproduced itself, in an evolutionary process of technology production adaptation and consumer market selection.

The source of capital for new investments is from previously successful entrepreneurial ventures.

The capital gain profit generated in the "exit" events of those earlier ventures serves as the source of capital for later ventures.

Applying Schumpeter's insights to the new world order corporatist economy, means that if entrepreneurs cannot obtain investment capital to start new ventures, then the pattern of economic growth stagnates at a low level of activity, as it did in Sweden.

Schumpter wrote,

"The entrepreneur needs capital…to serve as a fund out of which productive goods can be paid for…it is a fund of [future] purchasing power."

The entire entrepreneurial economic growth process begins with a fund of capital that can be invested by an entrepreneur.

He wrote,

"It [entrepreneurial profit] attaches to the creation of new things, to the realization of the future value system…Without [entrepreneurial] development, there is no [entrepreneurial] profit, and without profit, no [economic] development…without [entrepreneurial] profit there would be no accumulation of wealth."

The new entrepreneurial firms, for Schumpeter, represent the demand for capital, while the capital from the exit events represents the supply of capital.

In Schumpeter's economic model, there is a circular flow between buyers and sellers, which creates an internal dynamic force in the economy.

"…sellers of all commodities appear again as buyers in sufficient measure to acquire those goods which will maintain their consumption and their production equipment in the next period at the level so far attained, and vice versa."

Schumpeter described the concept of an economy breaking away from an old equilibrium point as,

"...a discontinuous change in the channels of the [circular] flow... a disturbance of equilibrium, which forever alters and displaces the equilibrium state previously existing economy...These spontaneous and discontinuous changes in the channel of the circular flow and these disturbances of the center of equilibrium appear in the sphere of industrial and commercial life, not in the sphere of the wants of the consumers of the final product."

In Diagram 2, we update Schumpeter's explanation of an economy breaking away from equilibrium to add that an economy in a low level of activity may not be able to break away from a status quo equilibrium, as was the case of Sweden, after 1980.

An economy that is stuck at a low level of economic aggregate demand is called a "Nash equilibrium."

We explain that since 1980, the economy of Sweden, and all other European socialist nations, have been stuck in a Nash equilibrium, caused by the lack of economic growth in the global corporate crony capitalist system.

We further allege, that since the economic collapse of 2008, in the United States, that the U. S. economy has been stuck in a national low-growth, Nash equilibrium.

We argue that the way out of the Nash equilibrium is a new form of entrepreneurial capitalism that creates new future markets.

Diagram 2. Economy Breaking Away From Equilibirum to a Nash Equilibrium.

Diagram 1. Economy Breaking Away From Equilibrium In Time Period One to Potential Attractor Point of Economic Decline in Time Period Two.

According to Schumpeter, an economy is either growing or it is dying, and there is no theoretical reason to assume that the direction of the economy is always upward to a new growth point equilibrium.

Nor, is there any theoretical reason to believe that the economy returns to the prior equilibrium point after an economic collapse, or after economic growth stops.

When Schumpeter explains that the disturbances are in the sphere of industrial life, and not in the market of final demand, he is describing the function of the intermediate demand markets, the inter-industry supply chain linkages, which change forever as a result of technological innovation.

The intermediate demand and final demand markets change forever because the economic structure resulting from capital investments are different than the previous economic structure.

Schumpeter explained that the allegiance of the ruling social class to the status quo arrangement of political power in the economy would cause the economic growth to stagnate at lower levels of aggregate demand in the absence of new capital investment.

The business-social networks that Schumpeter identified with monopoly capital were comprised of old production units, commercial bankers, institutional money, and senior management of branch plants of multi-national corporations.

Schumpeter explained that this corporate network had financial interests in maintaining the social class status quo distribution of income because uncertainty over loan repayments to commercial bankers upset the flow of benefits that the ruling class achieves from the status quo arrangement of power.

The social conflict, as described by Schumpeter, is that bankers depend on stable flows of revenue from the borrowers to repay their loans, and thus, choose only to fund the most cautious and stable of enterprises that come before the bank's loan selection committee.

The most cautious and stable firms are primarily existing, established firms, that are plugged into the business-social networks, not new ventures and startups, that do not have the right business or family connections to obtain a loan.

In Schumpeter's economic model of 1935, commercial bankers,

"... supplied the entrepreneurs with purchasing power by furnishing them with credit. Moreover, because bankers are not able to create credit in unlimited quantities, [before 1992], they have to select from among the investment plans put forward by entrepreneurs that they regard as desirable or likely to succeed."

Schumpeter continued,

"The direction that the economy will follow will depend on the investment plans that are chosen by the bankers, and therefore, it is bankers who constitute the selection committees for investment plans; they are the helmsmen of the capitalist economy."

We agree with Schumpeter that global institutional bankers are the helmsmen of the new world order, and update his definition of commercial bankers to apply to modern global investment banks and central bankers.

Schumpeter explained that the political resistance to the new products and new technology being used by new firms was in the form of political allegiance to maintaining the status quo distribution of income between the ruling class and common citizens.

Existing firms, and existing commercial bankers, who may have loaned money to those established firms, have a motivation to control the direction of technology in order to eliminate potential future competition from new ventures, in order to maintain their incomes.

The status quo rate of interest of loans made by commercial bankers tends to establish the prevailing rate of interest for the commercial bankers, based upon their assessment of risk.

The prevailing rate of interest acts as the target benchmark for all commercial bankers in assessing the risks and profitability of a new loans in either a new firm, or an established, existing firm.

For Schumpeter's theory of economic growth, it is income competition between two social classes that is the major dynamic in explaining economic growth rates.

Schumpeter explained,

"Every individual loan transaction is a real exchange...the exchange of present for future purchasing power...the *control* [italics added for emphasis] of present purchasing power means more future purchasing power [more income] to the borrower…For what business yields interest [profits] permanently? The return [from operational profits] of every business ceases after a time, for every business, if it remains unchanged, and soon falls into insignificance...According to our view, the capitalist [banker] would first have to lend his capital to one entrepreneur, and after a certain time period to another, since the first cannot be permanently in the position to pay interest."

Schumpeter's essential point, as it relates to economic evolution, however, was that product technology evolves as a process of disequilibrium, not equilibrium, and that the economic evolution itself is also an auto-correlative cause of further disequilibrium because each evolutionary transition results in a new economic structure.

We update Schumpeter's analysis of disequilibrium to include a national Nash equilibrium that ratchets downwards, as the macro economy slowly collapses, as a result of the absence of the social distribution of benefits from technological innovation.

Schumpeter understood that under conditions of monopoly capitalism, the benefits of the free market competition will not be distributed throughout all social classes.

Schumpeter thought that the lure of monopoly profits was so strong that monopoly capitalism would eventually overwhelm the forces of free market competition.

In order to achieve monopoly profits, Schumpeter predicted that the corporations would adopt two strategies which would reduce the pace of technical change.

First, the corporations would attempt to integrate backwards, into the sources of supply for production. By buying up their suppliers, or creating subsidiaries to compete with the existing suppliers, the corporations could achieve a steady supply of intermediate goods, at costs that were controlled and predictable.

The control over the supply chain would mean that declining marginal costs of production could be more readily realized than if supply costs were variable and uncertain.

Second, because the marginal rates of profit increased with increased output, it became important for corporations to gain control over the unpredictable future demand at a price that corporations controlled.

The monopoly corporations had an urge for forward integration, into their sales and distribution channels. Their urgency was motivated by a desire to transform the declining marginal costs in mass global production into increasing marginal profits of mass global sales.

It was the consequences of this forward and backwards integration of global corporations that made Schumpeter pessimistic about the future.

He believed that the corporations would achieve the power to determine the future markets, independent of consumer choices.

He thought that the corporations would internalize the process of technical change, through control over research and development, in order to manipulate consumer demand, and control production costs to suit their own private financial interests.

He was concerned that the dominant powerful global firms would limit technological innovations within their corporate structure in order to reap greater profits from their status quo monopoly position.

Schumpeter feared that significant technological innovations would only occur in large multi-national corporations that had sufficient resources to conduct extensive research and development.

Schumpeter went even further by describing that the crony capitalist relationship between commercial bankers and corporations tended to compound the negative effect on the pace and direction of technical change.

Schumpeter was concerned that if bankers formed a political alliance, in a 2-party representative republic, with monopoly corporations, that the flow of investment capital to new ventures would be controlled as a result of crony corporate capitalism.

Schumpeter's term for monopoly global capitalism was "corporatism."

In his evolutionary model, the early phase of entrepreneurial capitalism would lead to corporatism and to a one world government political system disconnected from either democracy, or free consumer choice, in the final demand market.

Under global monopoly corporatism, the direction and creation of technology is controlled by a small set of corporations, and investment in technology innovation is a crony capitalist politically controlled and manipulated system that displaces the free price competitive market environment.

J. R. Hicks, in Value and Capital, [1939], noted that under conditions of price competition, equilibrium can be reached, theoretically, if firms face rising marginal costs in production.

In the face of declining marginal costs, firms may be able to achieve economies of scale in operation, leading eventually to monopoly.

He went on to note that,

"...the only reason why marginal costs should increase is the increasing difficulty in controlling production and marketing in the enterprise, as the scale of production grows."

In other words, the implementation of globalism, following Hicks, should have been followed by increasing marginal costs, which were caused by increasing difficulty in controlling the supply chains, as the global scale of operations increased.

As we argue, as a result of the implementation of internet communication technology, [ICT], beginning around 1992, the global production process means that a corporation in any part of the world can manage and control production in any other part of the world, instantaneously.

As a result of using ICT, any corporation in the developed world can take advantage of slave labor in China to gain declining marginal costs of production, and gain increasing marginal profits in the developed world by selling cheap Chinese goods at a high retail price in developed nation-states.

Chapter 2. Declining Marginal Costs of Global Production in the New World Order Macrotechnology.

We update Schumpeter's gales of creative destruction by adding the new factor of production of internet communication technology [ICT] to Schumpeter's analysis of the trends towards global monopoly corporatism.

When the global crony corporations in the U. S., off-shored the intermediate demand supply chains to China and India, they permanently, and deliberately, damaged the American initial factor endowment of individual enterprise for creating new entrepreneurial ventures.

With the fall of the Berlin Wall, in 1989, the crony corporation's political leadership realized that an opportunity existed to expand production and sales, around the globe.

Richard D. Wolff, in his Salon article, "How racism became the essential tool for maintaining a capitalist order," explains that the large U. S. corporate leadership had a type of collective "eureka" moment. [Salon, June 26, 2020.].

Wolff writes,

"So in this eureka moment capitalists said, "What are we doing here in Western Europe, North America and Japan? It's much more profitable if we produce in China, India and Brazil." And there begins what we're still in the middle of: the exodus, the abandonment of the places of origin of capitalism by the capitalists. If you go from high wages in the United States to low wages in China, the bottom line is that the people earning wages are earning a lot less than they used to. It's not just that they're not Americans; they're Chinese, but they can't buy back what you're building."

After this eureka moment, U. S. monopoly capitalism transitioned to global corporate cronyism.

The initial stages of global corporatism involved innovative ways for large corporation to move production facilities to low cost nations. [Laurie Thomas Vass, Searching for Signs of Technological Innovation in the Ruins of the American Economy, August 4, 2008. Available at SSRN].

In other words, the corporations reached a collective decision that domestic U. S. sovereign interests were not relevant or significant, to global operations. The corporations began the process of seeing themselves as "citizens of the world," not citizens of the United States, with duties and obligations of citizenship to the sovereign economic interests of all citizens in the nation.

At that time, the technology of internet communication technology was not sufficiently advanced to allow corporations to move operations to every part of the world.

They began, in 1992, with NAFTA, to move low-wage manufacturing production to Mexico, which was close enough geographically to manage and control both production of cheap goods in Mexico and sales and marketing at high retail prices in the U. S. and Canada.

From 1992 to 2001, the improvements in internet communication technology evolved and improved to the point where global corporate management became more efficient.

As ICT improved, it became more practical for U. S. corporations to include China in the new world order production scheme.

The major political forces behind admitting China to the World Trade Organization, in 2001, were U. S. domestic corporate political agencies, in their crony capitalist function in the rent-seeking U. S. political system. [Who Is It In America That Is Responsible For Implementing the Trade Agreements With China? Laurie Thomas Vass, CLP News Network, March 2022.].

When global corporations adopt ICT as an input factor of production, the ICT improves internal productivity, but also affects the dynamics of global market competitive conditions, because all global corporations are also simultaneously adopting the same technology.

The major management policies that change as a result from the adoption of ICT in global corporations can be summarized as:

- Restructuring to the core technological competency, with ensuing layoffs and downsizing.
- Outsourcing components of the supply chain manufacturing process, relying upon small, flexible, highly automated manufacturing firms, primarily located in major metropolitan areas of the world and adapting a just-in-time inventory supply process.
- Adapting to fast product cycles, and very limited response times to changes in market demand, made possible by the communication networks of the new information communication technology [ICT].

Protecting the core technological competency or extending that core competency along compatible new technology paths for new products became the focus of global corporations.

By restructuring, and layoffs to middle managers in the U. S. domestic market, the senior global corporation executives cut themselves off from the source of internal learning and tacit new knowledge.

Prior to 1992, the senior managers discovered technical changes through tacit knowledge about their interindustrial trading partners from middle managers.

The middle managers were the most important resources of institutional corporate knowledge of existing markets and technology because they were the staff located closest to the production process, and had the widest network of business professionals in the supply chains.

Prior to 1992, it was a result of being located within a specific geographical intermediate demand input-output network that enabled the global corporation to "know and learn" about technical change as it relates to the corporation's core competency.

The macro economic consequences of using ICT as a factor of production were statistically significant increases in U. S. productivity.

The productivity data described in U. S. government reports, after 2001, however, did not show theoretically-expected job increases.

This would be called a theoretical anomaly in economic equilibrium theory because productivity improvements are always accompanied by job increases in that theoretical tradition. [Thomas Kuhn, The Structure of Scientific Revolutions, University of Chicago Press, 1962.].

In 2015, Larry Summers called this theoretical anomaly the "productivity puzzle."

He stated,

"On the one hand we have enormous anecdotal evidence and visual evidence that points to technology having huge and pervasive effects. Whether it is complementing workers and making them much more productive in a happy way, or whether it is substituting for them and leaving them unemployed can be debated. In either of those scenarios you would expect it to be producing a renaissance of higher productivity…the productivity statistics on the last dozen years are dismal. Any fully satisfactory view has to reconcile those two observations and I have not heard it satisfactorily reconciled." [Tim Worstall, Larry Summers And The Productivity Puzzle, Forbes, Feb 21, 2015.].

The productivity puzzle had been evident in the U. S. economy, as a result of the advent of computer integrated manufacturing, in the mid-1970s. After the advent of computer integrated manufacturing, the productivity puzzle became a bigger anomaly because of the absence of job growth statistics, primarily in the manufacturing sectors.

In an effort to better understand the American productivity puzzle, the National Science Foundation commissioned a research project and retained Marc Uri Porat to conduct the investigation.

His report, The Information Economy: Definition and Measurement, provides a useful intellectual framework for explaining the so-called theoretical anomaly that is caused by the adoption of global information communication technology. [Marc Uri Porat, The Information Economy: Definition and Measurement, Washington, D. C: U. S. Department of Commerce, O. T. Special Publication 77-12[1]. 1977.].

His method of investigation placed ICT within the framework of an econometric input-output model [I-O] in order to explain how ICT in one sector affects other industrial sectors.

His logic in using the input-output model is that,

"Most information markets require a chain of output from other information industries in order to deliver the final product."

Porat began his investigation by defining internet information flows within an economy in terms of knowledge flows between different industrial sectors. In his framework, a corporation must be able to turn internet information into technological knowledge about how things work.

Deriving knowledge from internet information flows is not an easy task, and not a given outcome because gaining knowledge requires a prior intellectual construct to interpret the information, and internal corporate staff capable of turning raw data into useful knowledge.

As Porat points out,

"One of the most difficult [and lucrative] problems in an information rich world is developing skills to package information that is useful: in the right form, at the right place and the right time."

Porat's application of I-O is slightly different in its intent than the conventional use of I-O, which generally focuses on the impact that a change in final demand will have on intermediate demand, also known as income multiplier analysis.

In Porat's case, he is using I-O to trace information flows from the start of the production process to final demand for finished goods, rather than as the conventional case of starting with final demand and working back towards the start of the production process, with raw supplies.

This logical chronological sequence, that Porat calls the "chain of output," allows for a better understanding of what ICT is, from a static equilibrium perspective.

Porat describes and categorizes firms in relationship to their connection to the "information as knowledge" flows in the economy.

His three classes of information are:

Markets *for information*, which consists of firms that produce knowledge or innovations.

Information in markets, which consists of firms that are oriented to the search and coordination function within markets.

Information processing and transmission infrastructure, which consists of firms which provide the technological networks upon which information flows.

Porat's classification scheme allows the different effects of ICT, as described as a factor input to production, to be distinguished between the technical engineering networks of computers, routers, gateways, etc., and the social/business networks of the managers and workers who use ICT in the transformation of information to internal corporate knowledge.

When information communication technology is viewed as a factor of production in an input-output relationship, it is easier to imagine how information, as an input, enters a production process, wherein something happens on the input side, and knowledge comes out as an output.

ICT, as seen as an input, has a simultaneous analog with other factors of production. In the case of ICT, the output is knowledge, while in the case of other factors of production, the output is increased productivity.

The input-output conceptual framework, deployed in conjunction with Porat's definition of "information as knowledge" flows, allows Porat to ask two important questions about how computer integrated manufacturing affects corporations:

First, how does internet inter-industry information flows affect a firm's knowledge about existing markets.

Second, given a fixed production function, a fixed profit maximization objective function, in a given period of time, how does current knowledge about markets affect a firm's decisions about the level of production, the type of production, and the type of finished product to produce in the next period of time.

The dilemma for global corporations, in managing global operations, according to Porat, is that senior managers,

"...must await the decision of the marketplace [in the current period of time] before they can determine the level of output for the next period of time."

In the globalist production setting, technological knowledge about production is occurring in China, and the decisions about the verdict of the market are taking place in high income nations.

The dilemma that U. S. corporations confront in the global setting is that the information-to-knowledge flows in the supply chain are truncated.

The Chinese managers of U. S. production plants in China are in a better position to turn internet information into knowledge than U. S. senior executives, located in the United States.

The superior advantage that the Chinese managers obtain about production technology is one reason why China has been so successful in obtaining proprietary technological knowledge from U. S. products, which are produced in China.

The Chinese managers see the verdict of the final demand market at the same time as U. S. executives, but the Chinese managers have a "first-to-market" advantage over U. S. corporations in applying technological knowledge to production units in China.

Porat's conceptual I-O framework draws out this dilemma because ICT allows all competitors to see and implement a new production technology at the same time, after it has already been implemented by the Chinese managers.

The superior position of the Chinese managers allows them to be "first-to-market," because they are the first ones to convert internet information into knowledge.

This is the distinction between what ICT is and what it does as a factor of production. Technology is the application of knowledge, and ICT is the technical network that connects information flows to knowledge.

When U. S. corporations moved manufacturing operations to China, after 2001, they cut themselves off from the most important tacit knowledge gained from the intermediate demand markets of ICT.

The input-output relationship between information and knowledge is contingent in the output of knowledge. The contingency creates uncertainty within the firm at the same moment that information flows across industries are creating market instability.

Part of the uncertainty and instability for U. S. senior executives is related to ICT as a technical factor of production and part of it arises from what ICT does in terms of the mental transformation of information into knowledge, within the corporate structure.

As Porat's analytical framework points out, being connected to the internet is not the same thing as automatically deriving knowledge from the connection. Deriving knowledge, in the case of the global corporation is essential for handling the uncertainty created by the unstable global markets.

Porat's use of an input-output model that describes information flows between industrial sectors was also useful for understanding the "productivity" puzzle confronted by Larry Summers.

The puzzle is that productivity improvements occur in U. S. manufacturing plants located in China, and the data on increased productivity shows up in U. S. government statistics as improvements in productivity, as if the U. S. economy experienced productivity improvements in the domestic U. S. economy.

The productivity improvements were achieved with no increase in the U. S. manufacturing labor force because the U. S. corporations shifted employment growth to China, when they shifted supply chains to China.

The expected income and employment multiplier effects from productivity improvements occur in China, not in the domestic U. S. economy. The economic statistics show up in U. S. economic reports, but not increased employment numbers related to productivity improvements.

The long term damage to the U. S. economy resulting from globalism is not simply lower domestic rates of job growth and economic growth. The damage is related to the loss of information-as-knowledge gained in the information flows in the supply chains, now located in China.

One of the main effects of the application of ICT on the operations of large U. S. corporations is to reduce the costs of administering the corporation, no matter how large or how geographically dispersed it may be.

A global firm that introduces ICT faces declining marginal costs in the command and control functions of administration. The increasing scale of operation, and the declining marginal costs caused by ICT as a factor of production, are accompanied by drastic restructuring, downsizing in the domestic U. S. economy, and an extreme corporate focus on protecting the firm's core technical competency.

Globalism allows U. S, corporations to obtain declining marginal costs of production by placing the production process in low wage countries, thus contributing to the forces of Schumpeter's monopoly global corporatism.

In order to maintain the advantages of global crony capitalism, the U. S. corporations require a political crony capitalist new world order to protect their status quo distribution of income that benefits the welfare of the corporations, and not the social welfare of the U. S. middle and working classes.

Chapter 3. The Failure of New World Order Globalism in Promoting National Economic Growth and Shared Prosperity.

Harvard economist George Borjas estimated that open borders and global trade reduced the wages of American citizens by an estimated $118 billion a year. [Immigration Economics, Harvard University Press, 2014.].

At the same time that American workers are losing $118 billion a year, the open borders global economy generates a net increase in profit for U. S. global corporations of $128 billion a year.

The increased profits are counted as a surrogate for increased productivity, in the government reporting methodology, because the increased profits were gained by a decrease in labor cost inputs.

Output increased with reduced labor cost inputs, albeit, the increased production occurred in China.

Susan Houseman, of the Upjohn Institute, provides an example of why the GDP statistics mask the weak domestic economic growth.

She explained that the $100 million price drop from intermediate inputs from China displaces $150 million in U.S. domestic economic activity, but the GDP data cannot capture that economic loss. [Susan Houseman, Understanding the Decline of U.S. Manufacturing Employment., Upjohn Institute for Employment Research, 2018.].

Houseman states,

"The greater the share of imported intermediates going into an exported good or service, the fewer domestic jobs will be generated. So clearly it's important to be able to quantify the use of imported intermediates in, say, an exported piece of construction equipment. But the existing data yields no clue about whether export-oriented industries use more or fewer imported intermediates, relative to industries that principally produce for domestic markets."

The increased profits of global corporations is accompanied by a reduced payback period for any new product created by corporate R & D, and reduces the length of time existing sustaining product innovations remain profitable.

The new dynamic of the global market requires any single corporation to be first to market, with a sustaining innovation, and then first to market again, with a second round of sustaining innovation, in the immediate future period of time.

Other corporations immediately see the profits being made by the first to market corporation, and copy the sustaining innovation.

The Chinese managers of U. S. production plants located in China, have an advantage in turning the subsequent sustaining innovations into products that mimic the new innovation because they are closest to the production process.

Many of these Chinese companies have become what can be considered as "national" champions for China in the global economy.

The majority of these "champion" companies are among China's largest global companies and many are state-owned enterprises (SOE).

The SOEs' mission is to support China's rise as a global super power. Currently, 98 of the Chinese companies listed on the Fortune Global 500 list are state owned, including China's 12 largest companies.

Recognizing that technological innovation plays a significant role in economic growth, the Chinese government introduced policies promoting domestic innovation in 2006.

Today, 42% of total profits claimed by publicly traded SOEs can be attributed to 20 companies, most of which are in protected sectors such as oil, steel and utilities. [Antonio Graceffo, China's National Champions: State Support Makes Chinese Companies Dominant, Foreign Policy Journal, May 15, 2017.].

The Communist Party government commands government departments to give preference to domestic firms when selecting bids for government contracts

In certain industrial technology sectors, there are specific regulations banning foreign companies from entry unless the foreign patents are filed and held in China. [codified knowledge].

In other instances, foreign companies are banned from entry unless they agree to a technology transfer over to a local Chinese partner

After 2001, American corporations developed a symbiotic collaboration with the Chinese government that resulted in the competitive technological advantage of Chinese corporations, through deliberate technology transfer.

The U. S. corporations willingly, and willfully, agreed to turn American-made technology over to the Chinese government, in exchange for the short-term profits gained from production using low-cost slave labor in China.

As a result of Honeywell's technology transfer efforts, China stole the technology for its nuclear warheads, including Honeywell's guidance systems for the W-88 warhead capable of delivering 150 Kilotons within 80 yards of it intended target.

China stole from Honeywell the technology for testing these warheads through simulations and firing in camouflage mode.

China obtained from Honeywell the software for radar detection of operating attack submarines.

Under the trade agreements promoted by the Business Roundtable, China is using Honeywell's avionics and aircraft technology to build the new Chinese commercial jet, the C919.

Chinese crony state communism could not function without the symbiosis of profits from American global corporate crony capitalism.

And, American globalist crony capitalism could not reap short-term profits and function without the Chinese communist model.

When the large U. S. corporations moved their regional intermediate supply chains to China, around 2002, they disconnected themselves from allegiance to the national economy, and functioned more as "citizens of the world" than American corporate citizens.

As Leonard Lynn and Hal Salzman note in "Collaborative Advantage,"

"U. S. multinationals are weakening their national identities, becoming citizens of the countries in which they do business and providing no favors to their country of origin. This means that the goal advocated by some U.S. policymakers of having the United States regain its position of leadership in all key technologies is simply not feasible, nor is it clear how the United States would retain that advantage when its firms are only loosely tied to the country." (Issues In Science and Technology, Winter 2006).

The global corporate allegiance is to the global alliance with the Chinese Communist Party, facilitated by a corporate political lobbying agency called, the U.S. China Business Council.

Both the US China Business Council and a second corporate lobbying agency, called the Business Roundtable, are primarily responsible for implementing the trade agreements with China, and for writing the subsequent legislation that allows American companies tax-advantaged benefits from production in China.

The USCBC is a private, nonpartisan, nonprofit organization of approximately 200 American companies that do business with China.

As they modestly state on their website, the mission of the USCBC is to "Help Shape the World's Most Important Relationship."

Their membership overlaps with the members of the Business Roundtable, which provides added political muscle to implement their covert political activities in Washington.

About 75% of the 200 USCBC member companies are also members of the Business Roundtable, which has branch affiliates in major metro regions in the United States.

Diagram 3. lists a selection of the 200 American companies who are members of the USCBC.whose company names start with the letter "A."

Diagram 3. Selected U.S. China Business Council Member Companies, Names Starting With letter A.

3 M	ABB Inc.	Abbott Labs	AccuWeather, Inc.	Adobe Systems	Advanced Micro Devices.	AIG
Air Products and Chemica	Airbnb, Inc.	Akin Gump Straus	Albright Stonebridge Group	Alcoa Inc.	Allen & Overy LLP	Alston & Bird LLP
Amazon	American Express Company	Amgen Inc.	Amphenol Corp	Amway	Analog Devices.	APCO Worldwide

Diagram 4. is an abbreviated list of member companies and CEOs in the Business Roundtable, just to provide a sense of the overlap between the members of the two political lobbying groups.

Diagram 4. Selected Member CEOs and Companies of the Business Roundtable Whose Company Name Begins With the Letter A Who Are Also Member Companies of the USCBC.

Mike Roman CEO 3M	Robert Ford CEO Abbott	Shantanu Narayen CEO Adobe	Andy Jassy CEO Amazon	Peter Zaffino CEO American International Group	Tim Cook CEO Apple	Juan R. Luciano CEO Archer Daniels Midland

The full member list for the US CBC member companies is available on their website. https://www.uschina.org/

The full member list of companies in the Business Roundtable is available on their website. https://www.businessroundtable.org/

The Business Roundtable spent close to $10 million on lobbying members of Congress for Normal Trade Relation (NTR) passage, in 2001, at that time, the largest-ever political lobbying expenditure for a single special interest legislative issue.

Ordinary middle and working class American citizens, in 2001, did not have a comparable political lobbying agency to protect their financial interests.

As a consequence of the middle class political weakness, the two business lobby agencies were successful in damaging the social welfare of the middle and working class, while enacting legislation that benefitted the crony corporate class.

The research by Harvard professor George Borjas, cited above, shows a perfect symmetry between the $118 billion a year reduced the wages of American workers and the net increase in profit for U. S. global corporations of $128 billion a year, as a result of the global trade legislation.

The enigma of American crony capitalist corporations collaborating with communists is resolved by understanding that the crony Chinese state communism looks and functions just like American political system of crony corporate capitalism.

As Aligicia and Tarko explain, both the Chinese and American forms of cronyism can be categorized and placed into the larger framework of corporate global "rent-seeking."

They state,

"Our thesis is that (macro) crony capitalism is yet another type of rent- seeking society, (macro) crony capitalism is not mere rent-seeking, it is a meta-rent-seeking mechanism for securing the rents at consistently high levels…it as a quasi-technical label meant to describe a political system rife with corruption." (Huber 2002; Haber 2002). (Paul Aligicia and Vlad Tarko, Crony Capitalism: Rent Seeking, Institutions and Ideology, Kyklos, May 2014).

The three main components of both the American global crony national economic structure and the Chinese communist economic structure are:

1. The global firms in the military-industrial complex.

2. The global manufacturing industrial firms with a financial interest in obtaining foreign trade benefits, especially with China.

3. The global banking and investment firms who coordinate global financial transactions in conjunction with global central banks.

The common characteristics of global cronyism, in both economies, is a preference for collectivist globalism, as opposed to promotion of a sovereign national economic interest, and a preference for fascist political decision-making by the ruling class, as opposed to citizen participatory decision-making.

Like the top-down, one party political system in China, the American global corporate crony political system is a one party top down system, managed by the business lobbyist agencies, based in Washington, which functions entirely independent of the consent of the governed.

The one party ruling class in America looks like, and functions like, the CCP in China that directs economic wealth to the communist "national champion" cronies in the political system.

Todd Zywicki places U. S. corporate cronyism into an economic exchange framework to demonstrate that that the parties who benefit from the crony exchange exploit those who bear the costs of cronyism.

Zywicki states,

"In the (implicit crony) exchange, the firm promises to share some of that surplus with politically-favored groups, such as labor unions or favored interest groups (such as environmental groups), and with the politicians themselves through campaign contributions and other means of support. Thus, the firms and their managers and shareholders gain what amounts to a sinecure and protection from the gales of creative destruction, and in exchange politicians can divert some of this flow of resources to their preferred policies and groups. (Todd J. Zywicki, Rent-Seeking, Crony Capitalism, and the Crony Constitution, Supreme Court Economic Review, Forthcoming; George Mason Legal Studies Research Paper No. LS 15-08; George Mason Law & Economics Research Paper No. 15-26. August 26, 2015. Available at SSRN).

In 2013, U. S. corporations paid U. S. workers in manufacturing jobs an average of almost $34 an hour in wages and benefits, or a premium of almost 9 percent compared with all other American jobs, according to the Manufacturing Institute, an affiliate of the National Association of Manufacturers.

In China, after the trade deals were implemented, the U. S. corporations paid Chinese slave labor $200 per month, or just under $1 per hour.

The difference between $34 per hour and $1 per hour, in Marxian theory, is called surplus labor value, which was shared between U. S. corporations and the Chinese Communist Party.

The Wal-Mart trade deficit with China cost more than 400,000 American jobs from 2001 to 2013

Cisco now has 2,000 people doing R&D in India. Those jobs for highly skilled, highly-paid workers, used to be located in America.

In his article, Exposing the Roots of Globalism, in American Greatness, Theodore Roosevelt Malloch, explains that globalism is the advocacy of one world government, based upon the idea of democratic socialism and world citizenship. [Theodore Roosevelt Malloch, Exposing the Roots of Globalism, American Greatness, April, 2020.].

Malloch writes,

"Former UK Prime Minister Gordon Brown is using the Wu virus to call for a one world government. "Now is the time for global leaders to create one world government to tackle the twin medical and economic crises caused by the Chinese coronavirus pandemic," he urged on March 26, 2020."

In Davos, the global banking and financial system is coordinated with the needs of the global corporations to smooth out the uncertainty in global markets. The IMF implements the daily directives of the Davos agreements.

The Non Government Organizations, including the World Trade Organization, the IMF, the World Bank, and the United Nations, administer and manage the global corporate relationships.

The trade agreements with China were not a mistake, they were a deliberate policy choice by global corporations to implement an economic system that allowed them to use Chinese slave labor to reap enormous profits. (Laurie Thomas Vass, Who Is It In America That Is Responsible For Implementing the Trade Agreements With China?, CLP News Network. March 2020.).

We agree with the analysis of Curtis Ellis, in his article, China's Post-Virus Plan to Destroy America's Economy, where he states that,

"The "respected voices" calling for America to lift the tariffs on China [in 2019], are simply swallowing Beijing's sophisticated propaganda. China means to use this crisis to destroy us…Moreover, Beijing sees an opportunity in the pandemic to reverse President Trump's call to move manufacturing out of China. China's State Administration of Science, Technology, and Industry for National Defense (SASTIND), stated: "China will get more opportunities, including in the reduction of pressure for the international industrial chain to transfer away from China . . . The global epidemic has provided opportunities for improving China's international position and countering anti-globalization."

As a result of trade with China, there are less entry level jobs in upwardly-mobile industries in the U. S. that the young people can enter. Those occupational portals of entry were shipped over to China.

In the 1950s and 1960s, one part of the American economy that made America great was the stable jobs and internal career ladders that began with a private sector portal of entry into many high-wage occupations.

In that former era, the term "upward occupational mobility," characterized much of the American dream of working hard and getting ahead in society.

Manufacturing jobs were the single most important source of jobs that led to upward mobility because manufacturing jobs had such extensive employment multipliers in other industries.

Autor, Dorn, Hanson, et al. found that, when factory jobs disappeared, after 1992, that nothing showed up to replace them.

Displaced factory workers, and young people, have no entry points to the labor market. [David H. Autor, David Dorn, Gordon H. Hanson, The China Syndrome: Local Labor Market Effects of Import Competition in the United States, American Economic Review, October 2013.].

The reason that nothing showed up to replace the lost jobs was that the U. S. economic structure had been permanently damaged because the economy lost the ability to transmit the income and multiplier effects generated by manufacturing employment and production.

Moretti estimated that each additional manufacturing job, prior to 1992, in a city generated 1.6 nonmanufacturing jobs. [Enrico Moretti, Local Multipliers, American Economic Review: Papers & Proceedings, 2010.].

Moretti found even stronger multiplier effects of manufacturing for skilled jobs, in contrast to semi-skilled production jobs: an additional skilled manufacturing job in a city generates an estimated 2.5 jobs in local goods and services.

When the Business Roundtable was successful in moving manufacturing jobs to China, the entire occupation by industry matrix in the U. S. was destroyed, permanently.

The supply chains that used to transmit the multiplier effects disappeared, not because of automation and increased productivity, but because trade with China destroyed the income multiplier economic structure of the American economy.

The growth of the U.S. trade deficit with China between 2001 and 2017 was responsible for the loss of 3.4 million U.S. jobs, including 1.3 million jobs lost since 2008.

The permanent U. S. economic damage of new world corporatism as a result of trade with China is not simply the lost wages or the decline in social welfare of middle and working class citizens.

The corporate crony corporatism destroys the entrepreneurial capitalist dynamic of creating new technology ventures.

As the research by Decker, Ryan & Haltiwanger, et.al., [2017], indicate, since 2001, the U.S. entrepreneurial economy has not been growing like the period before the off shoring of intermediate supply chains began.

They state,

"The pace of business dynamism and entrepreneurship in the U.S. has declined over recent decades. We show that the character of that decline changed around 2000. Since 2000 the decline in dynamism and entrepreneurship has been accompanied by a decline in high-growth young firms." [Ryan A. Decker, John Haltiwanger, Ron S. Jarmin, Javier Miranda, Declining Dynamism, Allocative Efficiency, and the Productivity Slowdown, American Economic Review, May 2017.].

The reason for the weakness in new venture creation is that the American corporate crony capitalist system is damaging the rate of new venture creation and technological innovation in the major metro regions.

The recent International Monetary Fund [IMF] report, World Economic Outlook, examined the economic effect of 88 banking crises over the past four decades. They find that, on average, seven years after a bust, an economy's level of output was almost 10% below where it would have been without the crisis.

The national economies are not recovering to the economic levels of output attained in the earlier periods, before the bust. This economic failure, overtime, is not explained by general equilibrium theory, which predicts a return to the prior level of equilibrium after the bust.

Using Japan's economy as an example of the downward ratchet, from its economic crisis beginning in 1988, Japan's economy stagnated.

By 2002 Japan's output was almost 23% below its 1988 GDP.

In the U. S., private sector investment for equipment, intellectual property and structures began to decline in 1999. For 2010-2016, the average quarterly investment by business as a percentage of GDP was lower than it had been since the 1980s.

The number of small business firms created in the U.S. was actually lower in 2010 than 1999.

We argue that it this dynamic of Schumpeter's entrepreneurial economic growth theory that is the point of attack on the global new world order corporatism.

Chapter 4. Updating Schumpeter's Entrepreneurial Economic Growth Model As the Economic Alternative to the Corporate New World Order.

When an entrepreneur leaves the old unit to create a new venture, he goes through a process of guessing at prices in the future, and also guesses at the rate of profit to use in the spreadsheets for his business plan.

Old units provide some base line for these guesses, as far as they relate to cost of production.

The entrepreneur is the agent that links the unknown future of consumer preferences to technological possibilities, the result of which is economic growth.

In making the distinction between unknown prices and risks of the future, and the known costs and risks in the existing old production unit, Temin hits upon the single greatest economic contribution that entrepreneurs make to the evolution of technical change. [P. Temin, "Entrepreneurs and Managers," in P. Higonnet, D. Landes, and H. Rosovsky, [Eds.], Favorites of Fortune, Harvard University Press. 1991.].

Entrepreneurs perform the economic function of creating the future markets by imagining how that market will work.

They provide the guesses of future prices and profits, and how technological change in production units will interact with, as yet unseen, consumer preferences.

In contrast, the existing firm, is engaged in sustaining innovation, and does not create a future market, it adjusts itself to the prices and profits of the status quo market.

Existing products are on a pathway to technological obsolescence and declining marginal profits as new sustaining products become favored by consumers. As a result of the new world order, the product life cycle has become shorter.

Pier Saviotti describes where the entrepreneurs obtain their ideas for new ventures.

He writes,

"The knowledge of engineers, scientists, managers, technicians, etc., involved in the implementation of the technology becomes specialized around the process, technical and service characteristics used. This specialization creates networks of communication and power which reinforce the stability of the artifact dimension of the technology." [Pier Paolo Saviotti Technological Evolution, Variety, and The Economy, Edward-Elgar, 1996.].

When the entrepreneur leaves the old firm, he takes with him the tacit knowledge gained in "learning-by-doing," and also takes the network of personal relationships forged in the old firm.

In other words, an existing social-business network of skilled individuals, working in a production unit, share some specialized knowledge about a process.

Within this network, potential entrepreneurs meet with each other and discuss the feasibility of starting a new venture, based upon their technical knowledge and their understanding of the potential market for the products produced.

The entrepreneur provides an ingredient to the process of technical change that is absent in the framework of the existing old production unit, which is based upon codified knowledge.

According to Adams in Paths of Fire, the entrepreneurs have a "creative vision" in their capacity to anticipate a new convergence of consumer preferences and technological possibilities. [Robert Adams, Paths of Fire: An Anthropologists Inquiry Into Western Technology, Princeton University Press, 1996.].

Entrepreneurs come from the personnel ranks of existing production units.

Entrepreneurs have been involved in a number of collaborative relationships with their peers about how things work, and how to make things work better.

The entrepreneurs are a part of a social-business network, whose participants communicate with each other.

Entrepreneurs leave the old production units to create new ventures, using the knowledge they gained about how things work, and with ideas about how to make the new venture more productive than the older units.

The new ventures are more productive, and achieve higher overall production output per unit of input. Following Schumpeter, sometimes these new, entrepreneurial ventures blow the old firms away.

The accumulation of technological knowledge and the pace of technical change are contingent outcomes of the social and political institutional structure of a region.

For technological progress to occur, according to Joel Mokyr,

"...it must be born into a socially sympathetic environment." [Joel Mokyr, The Lever of Riches: Technological Creativity and Economic Progress, Oxford University Press, 1990.].

We argue that neither China, nor the current crony capitalist economy in the United States, possess the sympathetic environment for creating entrepreneurial technological ventures, after 2001.

The reason that the research by Decker, Ryan & Haltiwanger, describes a decline in the number of new ventures created in the U. S. after 2001, is that the new world order damaged the entrepreneurial sympathetic environment that existed in America.

The entrepreneurial American society constituted the initial factor endowment that provided the American economy with a comparative advantage over all other nations in the creation of new technological ventures.

The former American entrepreneurial social network acted to facilitate technical change, but was not organized as a special political interest group to defend its interests from the Business Roundtable or the USCBC.

The new world order business social network is well-organized, and well-financed to maintain the new world order.

The entrepreneurial social network constitutes a threat to the new world order because the uncertainty of a new radical innovation may upset the flow of benefits that they achieve from the new world order status quo arrangement of global power.

Following Schumpeter, there is a risk that the technological innovation of entrepreneurs may blow the old order away.

In response to the incipient threat of entrepreneurship, the global corporations starve the community of potential entrepreneurs for venture capital to start a new venture.

We agree with Schumpeter that the source of investment capital for new ventures, prior to 2001, was the capital gain exit profits from the venture, when it was sold or merged with another venture.

The strategy of the crony capitalist corporations was to eliminate this source of capital for investment, and to eliminate the free flow of tacit technological knowledge of potential entrepreneurs, if they left the old unit to start a new unit.

The pace of technical knowledge absorption generates a cumulative feedback mechanism that influences the path of economic development, via what W. W. Rostow has called the "plowback of profits for plant and equipment." [W. W. Rostow, The Process of Economic Growth, Norton & Co., 1962.].

In the case of the new world order, after 2002, the "plowback of profits" occurs in China's champion industries.

Schumpeter's insight into the maintenance of the monopoly capitalist social class status quo of the 1930's applies equally well to the current allegiance of American crony corporations to the status quo distribution of income in the new world order corporatist economy.

If large corporations can control the direction of technological change, then upward occupational mobility of the working and middle classes can be controlled.

If large corporations can control the creation and diffusion of tacit knowledge, then they can control the rate of new venture creation.

Technical change in the individualist model requires individual risk-taking, rewards based upon individual merit, and individual creativity.

If the new world order can make citizens dependent upon government welfare, then the individual initiative for risk taking for starting a new venture will be destroyed.

If the Federal Reserve Banks can bail out failed banks and corporations, after a collapse, then the risk of the new world order for the large global corporations is reduced.

For corporate and financial elites, the Fed's manipulation of the money supply and interest rates is seen as a tool to reduce risks on asset speculation.

The Fed's monetary policy acts as insurance to bail the elites out of the economic crisis that they create with their risky, speculative investments.

Schumpeter's geographically-decentralized entrepreneurial economic growth model is the only viable economic alternative to the tyranny of the new world order.

But, Schumpeter's entrepreneurial model must be updated to incorporate the political and financial tools that promote entrepreneurial capitalism.

Chapter 5. Adding Christensen's Analysis of Radical Disruptive Innovation to Schumpeter's Entrepreneurial Economic Growth Model.

Clayton Christensen made a distinction between tacit knowledge and codified knowledge, and suggested that large global corporations wanted to avoid open flows of tacit knowledge to protect the corporation's core technology. [Clayton Christensen, Efosa Ojomo, Gabrielle Gay, Philip Auerswald, How Market-Creating Innovation Drives Economic Growth and Development, Innovations / Blockchain for Global Development, 2019.].

Christensen's distinction about knowledge is important for understanding how Christensen's concept of open flows of tacit knowledge in blockchain innovation create new future markets that are not controlled in the new corporate world global economy.

Christensen writes,

"The ideas (or recipes) that are critical to market-creating innovation, and that actually propel growth and development, are overwhelmingly uncodified, context dependent, and transferable only at significant cost—which is to say that tacit knowledge dominates, information asymmetries [and] are the norm, [in new market creation] when transaction costs are significant."

Schumpeter also cited the creation of new markets as a threat to the status quo income distribution for global corporations.

Schumpeter wrote,

"One illustration of this process of combination is "the opening of a new market, that is a market into which the particular branch of manufacture of the country in question has not previously entered, whether or not this market has existed before."

Christensen notes that tacit knowledge is subject to "knowledge spillovers," because the diffusion of new tacit knowledge, in face-to-face communication, cannot be controlled by corporations.

He writes,

"Knowledge spillovers," refer to the free transmission of ideas that are non-rival and non-excludable. In contrast, a [codified] product [knowledge] is rivalrous if its consumption by one person precludes its consumption by another; it is excludable if access to it can be limited."

The diffusion of tacit technological knowledge poses a threat to global corporations because the new knowledge may lead to the creation of new products, and new flows of income in future markets that disrupt the new world order status quo.

In contrast to tacit knowledge, Christensen cites the importance of "codified" knowledge that is easier for the corporations to control with legal and proprietary barriers.

Codified knowledge is in the form of written documents, diagrams, schematics and written patents.

Tacit knowledge is in the form of face-to-face encounters between engineers and technical staff, and "learning-by-doing" on the production plant floor.

Codified knowledge generally leads to sustaining innovation, within the corporation's legal purview.

Sustaining innovations are improvements to solutions already on the market. They typically target existing customers who require better performance from a product or service.

Sustaining technology innovation does not cause the creation of new future markets, and does not cause economic growth because it uses existing assets and existing technology in a more efficient productive manufacturing process.

Christensen explains that the global corporation's extreme focus on sustaining innovation and codified knowledge makes the corporation vulnerable to radical innovations.

He writes,

"The large companies that had listened hard to customers and invested like crazy in new technologies still lost their market leadership when confronted with disruptive changes in technology and market structure."

In The Innovator's Dilemma, Christensen suggests that the first market appearance of new products cuts into the low end of the corporation's current marketplace and eventually evolves to the point where the new products displace high price and high-end competitors and the reigning technologies [of existing corporations]. [Clayton M. Christensen, The Innovator's Dilemma: When New Technologies Cause Great Firms to Fail, Harvard Business Press, 2016.].

Christensen's thesis is that large, global companies get blown away by radical innovation because of their extreme focus on existing customers, and their efforts to control the pace of sustaining improvements to existing products.

In other words, large corporations are committed to maintaining the existing technological status quo for as long as possible because that is how they make the most profits in the existing time period.

As applied to private corporations, Christensen argued that market leaders have difficulty diverting resources away from known customer needs in established markets, to the development of disruptive innovations, which often underperform established products in mainstream markets but offer benefits that potential new customers would value over existing products.

The dilemma for global corporations is that the status quo arrangement with existing customers makes it difficult to give up on them in order to focus on new customers that do not exist yet.

The potential new customers and new markets are a threat to existing corporations, but in a status quo environment, corporations are faced with declining marginal profits because all global competitors are implementing new production technology, at the same time.

In the mass, global market, unit sales may be stable or declining, but the early large marginal profit per unit is declining.

At the point of declining marginal profits, the product has become obsolete, and the product will not benefit from future sustaining innovation.

Christensen points out that the corporate allegiance to the status quo eventually means reduced gross profits in the upcoming reporting periods.

"Probably the most daunting challenge in delivering sales revenue growth," states Christensen, "is that if you once fail to deliver it, the odds that you will ever be able to deliver it in the future are very low."

The macro economic effect of the innovator's dilemma is that when the executives choose the status quo, the company is on a path to extinction, causing overall economic growth to decline.

As products become more standardized in their sustaining innovation technological features and more uniform in their production process, their marginal profit is headed to zero, and as the profit heads to zero, the rent-seeking political manipulation of the rules becomes more pronounced as income competition regarding maintenance of the status quo intensifies.

The corporations seek out advantages associated with tax incentives and gaining political authority to buy competitor companies with technology that complements the corporate core technology.

When global companies are blind-sided by the new competition, Christensen calls this phenomenon "disruptive technology." (Polaroid cameras disrupted by the cell phone, yellow book telephone pages disrupted by Amazon).

Diagram 5. describes the sequence of events in radical innovation, as seen from the threat to the global status quo of macrotechnology.

Diagram 5. Chronological Sequence of Events of a Radical Innovation Leading to A Potential Market Disruption.

Appearance of novel radical product from two-parent technology crossover.	Emergence of small niche market, as consumers select the new product.	Displacement of old product by new radical product. Product market micro bifurcation.	Creation of intermediate demand markets to support production and distribution of product.	Creation of new income flows where none had previously existed.	Profit reinvestment from capital "exit" events into technology trajectory created by new radical product.

In Seeing What's Next: Using Theories of Innovation to Predict Industry Change, Christensen argues that it is possible to predict which companies will win and which will lose in a specific situation. [Clayton Christensen, Seeing

What's Next: Using Theories of Innovation to Predict Industry Change, Harvard Business Press, 2004.].

"After a radical disruptive technology takes root in new markets," said Christensen, "and after new growth is created, disruption can invade the established market and destroy its leading firms."

As Christensen notes,

"The techniques that worked so extraordinarily well when applied to sustaining technologies, however, clearly failed badly when applied to markets or applications that did not yet exist."

Radical technology innovation is the cause of economic growth because radical innovation creates new future markets.

Under global crony corporate monopoly capitalism, the direction and creation of technology is controlled by a small set of corporations, and investment in technology evolution is politically controlled and manipulated event that displaces the free competitive market environment.

Chapter 6. Connecting Schumpeter's Entrepreneurial Innovation to Christensen's Economic Growth Tool of Blockchain Innovation.

Clayton Christensen cited the new blockchain technology as a tool to help promote economic growth, and we extend and modify his idea to include regional blockchains that go from idea creation to private securities exchanges for capital market transactions for private regional technology stocks.

We connect Christensen's concept of blockchain innovation to the concept of regional technology clusters, within which technology innovation occurs at the regional geographical level.

The concept of a geographically-specific technological cluster of industries is important understanding regional economic growth because the network of personal relationships in the cluster facilitates the technological absorption of technical change in a production process.

Morroni has described this existing set of firms in a region as,

"...a constellation of firms with a leading firm and a cluster of complementary organizations, or a network of independent firms with collaborative relationships...these collaborative co-operative linkages enable certain economies of scale to be achieved through high overall production volumes." [Mario Morroni, Production Process, Technical Change, Cambridge University Press, 1992.].

Absorption of tacit technological knowledge occurs as a result of a new production techniques being adopted by many firms located in the regional clusters, as a result of competitive imitation.

As the process of absorption of knowledge occurs, the regional economic structure of interindustry supply chains is modified to adapt to the new technology.

Blockchain drives economic development by enabling market-creating innovations, primarily in geographically specific regions because the diffusion of tacit knowledge is personal, and done mostly in face-to-face communications.

All of the engineers, scientists, mid-level managers in the regional clusters communicate with each other about how the new processes are working, and when they leave to create their own new venture, it is that new process that forms the basis on their own equipment and machinery purchases.

The entire process of regional technological innovation can be visualized and facilitated by Christensen's concept of using blockchain as a tool to promote economic growth.

Christensen writes,

"Blockchain is a public, decentralized, distributed digital ledger that is used to record electronic transactions. Each "block" in a blockchain contains specific information that cannot be altered, due to the distributed nature of the technology. In a blockchain-based economy, the market-creating innovation [new venture investment] and the institution governing it [social-business networks] are fundamentally intertwined." [Clayton M. Christensen, The Third Answer: How Market-Creating Innovations Drives

Economic Growth and Development, et al., Innovations, 2018.].

Christensen sees innovation as a dynamic way of life that continually modifies market institutions by opening up new markets and new occupational opportunities.

He states,

"Innovation is the process by which institutions that are critical to development emerge. It is through innovations that create or connect to new markets that societies can create jobs, pay taxes, and, ultimately, build strong and lasting institutions... From an economic development standpoint, innovations can be market-creating or sustaining, that improve [production] efficiency."

The reason one metro region develops a comparative technological competitive advantage over other regions, according to Saviotti is due to,

"...specific institutional configurations and by the cumulative, local, and specific character of the knowledge that the institutions possess." [Technological Evolution, Variety, and The Economy, 1966.].

The new markets created by technical change represent an entirely different economic structure, with its own internal dynamic of growth.

Product competition in the old units is based upon cost of production in the old units vis-a-vis other old unit age-peers.

Product competition in the old units affects consumer preferences for old unit products, but the prices used are not the same prices used for consumer preferences in new units, because the cost of production in new units is lower than old units, and the products, while having some common features, are different.

Chapter 7. The Blockchain Innovation Economic Growth Model of New Venture Creation.

The intent and purpose of the regional blockchain model of knowledge creation and diffusion is to increase the rate of new technology venture creation in the particular metro region.

A blockchain is, in the simplest of terms, a time-stamped series of immutable computer records of data that is managed by a cluster of computers not owned, or controlled, by a centralized organization.

The idea that the blockchain data cannot be owned, or controlled, by global corporations is one of the key strengths of the blockchain economic growth model.

Each of these blocks of data (i.e. block) is secured and bound to each other using cryptographic principles (i.e. chain).

The blockchain technology allows the entire process of regional new venture creation to be moved from physical interactions to internet collaboration.

The new venture creation process envisioned by the block chain model can be described as a series of "if-then" contingent statements, where any citizen in the region with an interest in economic growth could participate.

The series of "if-then" statements can be placed into a sequence of logical steps where the prior industrial structure of the region acts as the basis for predictions about future new venture creation:

• If exit events in the past create a pool of entrepreneurial profits, then if,
• The entrepreneurial profit is available to used to fund new ventures that create new products, then if,
• Consumers and markets select new products, then if,
• Complementary markets are created, then if,
• New patterns of income distribution are created, then if,
• New technological knowledge is created, then if,
• New technological knowledge is diffused, then if,
• New production assets are "called forth" from the expanding production possibilities frontier, the assets have a greater probability of being "inherited" by subsequent generations of products, and the evolution of the market can continue through a future attractor macro bifurcation and the emergence of an entirely new market.

At each stage of the "Then-if" logical process, the blockchan gates through the set of ideas that replicate the underlying new venture creation model of economic growth.

As described in Diagram 6, the entire process of new venture creation is envisioned to take place in a black chain network of computers, geographically located within 50 miles of the metro region.

Diagram 6. Regional Blockchain New Technology Venture Creation Model.

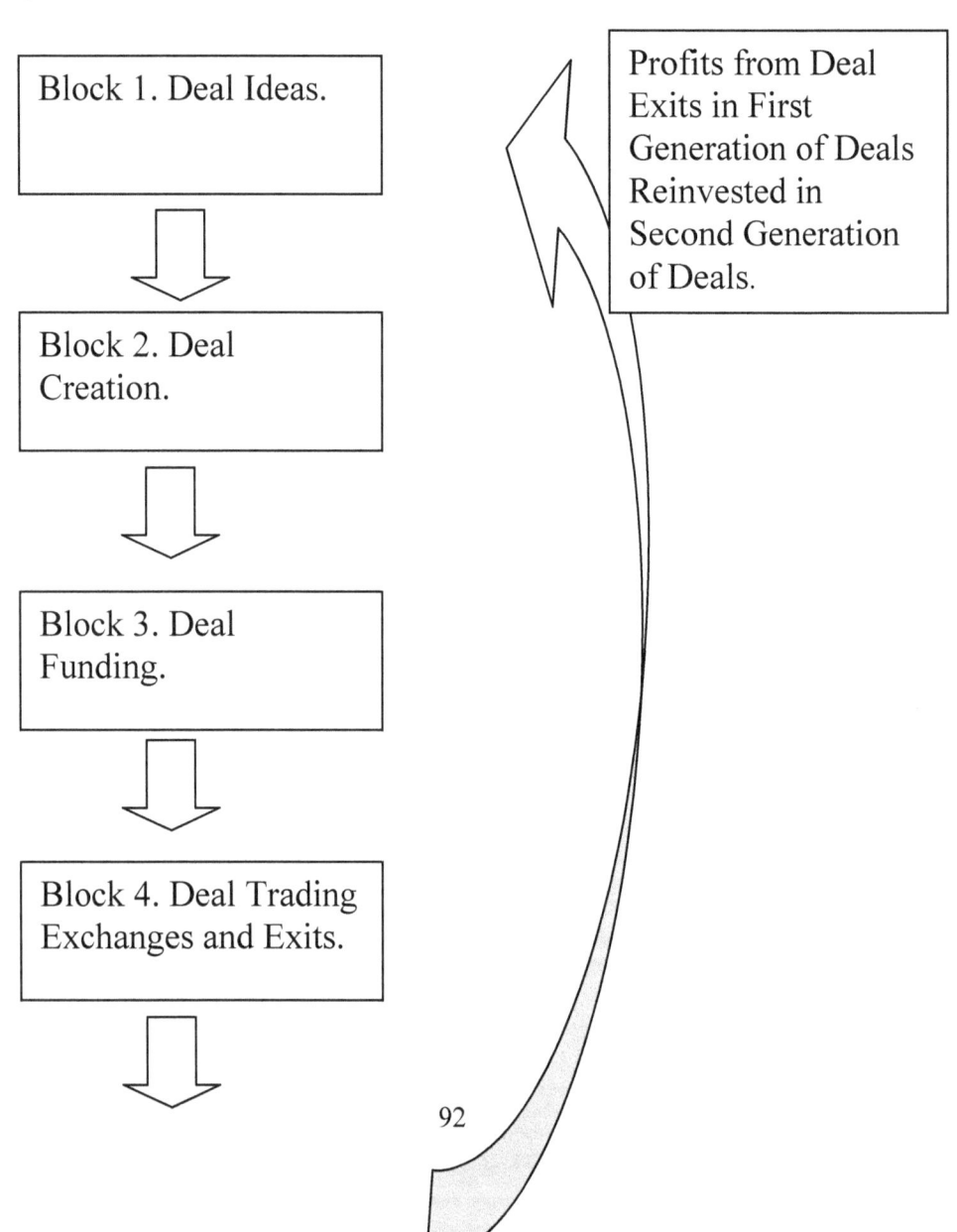

> Block 5. Deal Capital Gain Profits Reinvested in Next Generation of Deals.

ess network of engineers and engaging each other in block one to create and diffuse knowledge about potential new venture ideas.

The regional new venture creation blockchain is maintained by a peer-to-peer social network of people in the region who have an interest in new venture creation and regional economic growth.

The first block in the block chain is the organizing tool to bring the set of potential entrepreneurs together to collaborate on new venture ideas.

The communication in the first block supports and supplements the in-person, face-to-face networking events that currently occur in the entrepreneurial and angel capital forums, such as the events sponsored by the North Carolina Council for Entrepreneurial Development, in the Research Triangle.

In the first block of regional idea creation, any computer member on the node can add ideas and comment on other ideas for new ventures. This block is envisioned as an open forum to generate ideas for potential ventures that may work in that regional economy.

The block one network is a collection of both business and personal computers that are interconnected to one another. The individual computers take in data in block one, and add ideas that are seen by all participants.

The "peer-to-peer network" begins by partitioning the entire regional economy into technological clusters allow access by block on participants, who have a particular interest in that specific technological cluster.

Any computers in block one can add or modify their own contribution and data, with the ability to subsequently claim ownership of their new data or contribution.

Each "block" in a blockchain contains specific information that cannot be altered, due to the distributed nature of the technology. As a result, the blockchain technology has the potential to reduce uncertainty around ownership of new venture ideas and intellectual property rights and other property claims by providing verified records, and thereby strengthening private capital market institutions.

The intent and purpose of first block in the block chain is to facilitate communication among potential entrepreneurs who may not have previously known each other.

As Saviotti notes,

"...there is evidence from a number of studies to suggest that many of the important scientific ideas in the life of an innovation come from outside the innovating company, via these channels of professional scientific communication." [Rod Coombs, Paolo Saviotti, Vivian Walsh, Economics and Technological Change, Rowman and Littlefield, 1987.].

Ideas that gain community traction among participants in the first block are gated through to the second block for further processing into more definitive new venture ideas.

The communication in the second block brings in the set of professional advisors and other interested parties to view the progress of a potential new venture transaction.

In a process similar to current new venture business networking events, potential investors also have unlimited access to the shared data about a venture in the second block.

This process is commonly called "deal creation," where various legal and financial professionals collaborate with nascent entrepreneurs to refine the venture idea.

Any computer in the second block can freely contribute ideas and subsequently claim ownership of those ideas.

The nature of information changes in block 3 to be more like a private password protected set of computers.

The members with access to the third block would be potential private capital investors.

The new venture team would prepare a private placement memo to place online in the third block, and conduct both online and in-person forums for all interested investors, in order to present the venture concept and answer questions.

At the third stage of raising private placement capital for a new venture, the likelihood of corruption, misunderstanding, and administrative errors is significantly reduced when a transparent, distributed, and immutable system is used to manage the transfer of assets from one party to another

After the funding has taken place, only members who contributed private capital to the venture would be allowed access to on-going financial performance reporting on the progress of the ventures, in block four.

This periodic performance reporting would be somewhat like the 10-Q of listed public companies, but with less stringent auditing standards.

In the fifth, and final block, private investors could place bid and ask prices for the venture and transact secondary market exchanges.

If, and when, there was some type of exit event, the existing investors would be eligible to participate in the event, and would be offered new investment opportunities in subsequent new ventures.

In the case where there is no exit event, the investors can continue to monitor the performance of the venture, and continue to trade their ownership interests, in the closed, private stock exchange, much like they currently do in the pink sheets.

The initial partitioning of the regional economy into technology clusters is facilitated by an econometric tool, created by Professor Ed Feser. [Laurie Thomas Vass, Using Feser's Input-Output Model of Technological Affinities To Target Innovation Investments To Regional Industrial Value Chains, SSRN, 2008.].

Feser pioneered a modification in the conventional regional input-output analysis of regional economic structure. [E. J. Feser, and S. H. Sweeney, Industrial Complexes Revisited: A Test of For Coincident Economic and Spatial Clustering,

Working Paper, Department of City and Regional Planning, University of North Carolina, 1997.].

Feser's modification added the step of factor analysis to the national input output tables in the technical coefficients matrix, commonly called the A matrix.

The additional step of factor analysis allowed for the discovery of underlying technological affinities in manufacturing and production technology that exist between different industrial sectors.

Feser's factor analysis method results in the discovery of technological affinities that do not, on first glance, appear to be in obviously related regional industrial sectors.

Most cases of radical innovation involve the market commercialization of technology in products and services that are "new-to-the-world," and are not obvious.

This same idea of "shared specific knowledge" between what first appear to be unrelated industrial sectors was described by Bryce and Winter, as the "general inter-industry relatedness index." [David Bryce and Sidney Winter, A General Inter-Industry Relatedness Index, CES Working Paper 06-31, 2006.].

Bryce and Winter provide the example of the shared knowledge relatedness between the Metal and Partitions Sector, (SIC 2542), and the Automatic Vending Machines Sector, (SIC 3581), otherwise known as razor blades and drink machines.

The analytical results of the Feser and Bryce/Winters methods would suggest to entrepreneurs and private investors which industrial sectors in the region would be potential investment targets because they were "members" of the regional industrial clusters whose interindustrial multiplier relationships were not obvious.

The blockchain technology reduces the confusion and uncertainty that entrepreneurs face in the deal creation phase of new venture creation, that product development professionals call the "fuzzy front end."

As described in Diagram 6, the process of regional new venture creation, using blockchain computer technology, is intended to be an on-going process of profit reinvestment that creates self-sustaining, self-renewing regional economic growth, not controlled by global corporations who are intent on imposing the new world order.

Chapter 8. Exploiting the Vulnerability of New World Order Crony Corporatism.

The main propositions and assumptions of the advocates of the new world order can be summarized under the main heading that the economic growth generated in the nation-state model is inferior to the rate of economic growth that could be obtained under a corporatist new world order economic model.

Proponents of the new world order (NWO), do not refer to their economic model as globalism or global crony corporate capitalism.

Their term for the superior economic model is "shareholder capitalism," or alternatively "stakeholder capitalism." which functions much like the model of special interest negotiation between labor unions and large corporations, in Sweden, prior to 1980.

The subordinate propositions and assumptions of the new world order flow from this main initial assumption.

Diagram 7. presents the main propositions of the advocates of the NWO.

Diagram 7. New World Order Assumptions and Propositions.

Main Assumption: Economic growth in the nation-state model will not be sufficient to create jobs or employment for workers in all former nation-states.
- As a consequence of inadequate economic growth rates, the distribution of the benefits of economic growth will be limited to a few select nations.
- Citizen participatory democracy in the former nation-states cannot cope with global issues, like global warming. New global institutions are required to manage global trade and global economic growth.
- The Chinese model of global corporatism is superior to the nation-state model, and the transition to the Chinese crony corporate model is inevitable.
- American crony corporate capitalists will engage with Chinese crony corporate capitalists and the European Socialist crony corporations in negotiations over the correct distribution of income and global welfare benefits. The former free market decision–making model will be replaced by a "system of global financial interest representation." The common term to describe this decision making model is "corporatism."
- Internet Communication Technology (ICT) makes the global production model superior in economic production efficiency to national economic sovereignty, with China assuming the undisputed leader of the new world trading relationships.

The main propositions and assumptions of the advocacy of the new world order contain two false assumptions, which make the main propositions vulnerable to attack.

- The primary mistaken assumption is that Chinese global dominance is opposed by U S corporations, such as the 200 corporations of the U. S. China Business Council.
- The other mistaken assumption of the advocates of the NWO is that globalism will lead to higher rates of economic growth, whose distribution of benefits can be negotiated by the various special interests in the corporatist stakeholder model.

In the absence of tacit knowledge creation and diffusion, the rate of technological innovation will decline, world-wide. Without technological innovation, as Schumpeter, correctly stated, economic growth will decline, to a global Nash equilibrium.

The parties to the corporatist negotiation model will be left negotiating over a smaller and smaller global economic pie.

Klaus Schwab is the primary advocate for corporate globalism. In 1971, he founded the World Economic Forum, (WEF) which is the host organization of the annual conference on globalism in Davos, Switzerland.

Schwab is currently the Chief Executive Officer of the WEF organization.

In 1994, he published an extensive article in the Harvard Business Review, where he described the logic and propositions of the WEF. [Klaus Schwab and Claude Smadjav, Power and Policy: The New Economic World Order, Harvard Business Review, 1994.]

His initial arguments about the low rate of global economic growth echo the same logic of Larry Summers about the productivity puzzle.

To recap, in 2015, Summers, expressed being perplexed about how technological innovation could lead to global increased production efficiency, without causing global job growth.

Schwab noted in his 1994 article that,

"Observers have been speaking of a "jobless recovery" or a "recovery on crutches" because neither present nor projected growth rates are sufficient for creating jobs on a large scale. The hard truth is that growth in the industrialized countries will have to be greater than the 2.6% annual average of the last two decades for these nations to achieve a substantial reduction in their unemployment levels."

Schwab outlined the main assumption about the benefits of global corporatism, which we described above as,

"Economic growth in the nation-state model will not be sufficient to create jobs or employment for workers in all former nation-states."

Schwab writes,

"The hard truth is that growth in the industrialized countries will have to be greater than the 2.6% annual average of the last two decades for these nations to achieve a substantial reduction in their unemployment levels."

In other words, Schwab argues that the former economic nation-state model of economic growth of 2.6% GDP is insufficient to create global job opportunities, and that the global corporatist model could do better than 2.6%. growth, on a global economic scale.

Schwab argues that the Chinese model of global corporatism is superior to the nation-state model, and he argues that the transition from the nation-state model to the Chinese crony corporate model is inevitable.

Schwab writes,

"Perhaps the most spectacular component of the current revolution is the shift in the world economy's center of gravity to Asia…neither technology nor management and marketing techniques observe any boundaries, the key prerequisites of economic success are increasingly transferable from one country to another… Today, however, it is possible to have high technology, high productivity, high quality, and low wages. These competitive realities are creating intense pressure to rationalize production, cut internal costs, and search for the least expensive production base… [There is] an unspoken reluctance to acknowledge the end of Western supremacy and [that the industrial powers must] share economic power."

As we noted above, the logic of corporate globalism is based upon the implementation of ICT, which allows U. S. global corporations to combine production command and control in the U. S. with the slave labor of the Chinese society.

The value of this economic model, from the perspective of the member corporations in the USCBC, is the increased profits from slave labor in China, and the sales and marketing of the products in the high wage industrial nations.

Schwab describes that the participatory democratic decision making in nation-states is obsolete and must be replaced by a global corporatist negotiation model between global elites, such as the ones who meet every year in Davos.

He writes,

"A kind of "cultural revolution" will need to be instigated in the developed countries of the West in order to bring about the required adjustment, at the corporate and national levels, to the shift in economic power toward East Asia…The international institutions required to sustain, monitor, and supervise the new global economic order will need to be established or revamped as soon as possible."

Schwab extends and elaborates on his strategy for replacing representative republics with the stakeholder global fascist corporate model in his document, World Economic Forum's 2010 "Global Redesign."

He writes that,

"That a globalized world is best managed by a self-selected coalition of multinational corporations, governments (including through the UN system), and select civil society organizations…[Nation-state] governments are no longer the overwhelmingly dominant actors on the world stage and that the time has come for a new stakeholder paradigm of international governance."

In his most recent rendition of the global corporatist fascist model, in preparation for the 2022 WEF conference in Davos, Schwab is quoted in Breitbart News,

"In a world which is becoming more fragmented, more divided, and where many of the traditional multilateral organisations tend to become dysfunctional, or at least mistrustful, a global platform based on informal, trust-faced and action-oriented co-operation will be ever more relevant, more important than before," [Eve of Destruction: Klaus Schwab Pledges the World Can Find Salvation at Davos 2022, Breitbart News, May 19, 2022.].

The new global WEF economic platform is called "a circular economy," which conjures up images of Schumpeter's term, "the circular flow of economic life,"

Schumpeter argued that the equilibrium of a "circular flow" concept of economic growth did not guarantee that the economy would return to the prior equilibrium, after an economic disturbance knocked the economy out of equilibrium.

We extend Schumpeter's insight to allege that the WEF "circular economy," is a static, zero-sum, closed loop of economic activity among large corporations, which ends in a global Nash equilibrium.

The WEF explains that the circular economy requires the new corporate fascist state to regulate the wasteful consumer purchasing decisions under the current nation-state free market economy.

In preparation for the 2022 WF Davos Forum, the WEF writes,

[In the] the circular economy, technology drives down prices, [in production] which is good news. But as relative prices decrease, consumers tend to use more individualised transport, floor space and food. [consumer free choice]. In other words, the less stuff costs, the more we [individual consumers] want to use, eat **and waste it.** Policymakers acted quickly to avoid the potential environmental ricochet caused by increased prosperity." [emphasis added].

The main assumption of the WEF circular economy is that free consumer choice is wasteful and leads to global environment degradation. In their rendition, global warming requires a global fascist state to regulate wasteful consumer choice, as in the Chinese model of society.

They state in the WEF 2022 Davos preparation documents,

"Faced with the twin headwinds of increased CO2 emissions and increased resource extraction, the global economy is only 8.6% circular. Just two years ago it was 9.1%. The global circularity gap is therefore widening…In working with international organizations, [NGOs] including the World Business Council for Sustainable Development (WBCSD) and the Ellen McArthur Foundation, PACE [a WEF spin-off organization] is underscoring the importance of moving towards a common set of metrics to accurately measure global progress towards the circular economy."

Translated into real-speak, only 8.6% of the global economy is currently "circular." The other 91% of the world economy is not circular, and must, therefore be brought under WEF fascist corporate control to force the world economy to be circular.

The 2022 WEF Davos preparation documents end with this exhortation:

"The world needs a circular economy. Help us make it happen."

In order to make the world circular economy happen, the proponents of the new world order are calling for the "Great Reset," which would transition the institutions of sovereign nation-states to a global tyranny.

As Klaus Schwab notes, above, the Great Reset means that,

"That a globalized world is best managed by a self-selected coalition of multinational corporations, governments (including through the UN system), and select civil society organizations."

Schwab does not explain who it is, or what it is, that "selects the civil society organizations" that are to rule the world.

As Andrew Stuffaford writes in his National Review article, that the great reset would not be so dangerous if it were just a conspiracy theory. [Andrew Stuttaford, The Great Reset: If Only It Were Just a Conspiracy, National Review, November, 2020.].

Stuttaford wites,

"The 'Great Reset' masterminded by the World Economic Forum is just corporatism by another name…the common core conviction [of the WEF Great Reset] is that [global] society should be organized by and for its principal interest groups — let's call them "stakeholders" — intermediated by, and ultimately subordinate to, the state. The individual does not get a look in…It's something that Klaus Schwab, the WEF's founder and executive chairman, has been advocating for a long time."

When Stuttaford refers to the "state," he means that unelected, self-selected corporations replace the current institutions to implement global corporatism.

As explained by Peter Koenig, in his 2020 article, "Democracy" vs. Covid: A No-Go,"

"The Great Reset would be the total corporate takeover of all aspects of [global] life…the Great Reset involves using the global technocratic biosecurity state (otherwise known as the global public health system) to implement these changes. The end results will mean extensive restrictions on the physical environment around people, a forced digitization, and a loss of bodily autonomy (having a say in your own health decisions)."

The title "The Great Reset," was used by the WEF for the 50th annual meeting in June 2020.

The theme of the 2020 WEF meeting was rebuilding [Global] society and the economy following the COVID-19 pandemic. The theme of the 2022 WEF meeting is implementing "the circular economy."

The recent United Nations Global Pandemic Treaty, is the first step in transitioning nation-state sovereignty to global governance.

As we noted above in our propositions and assumptions about the New World Order,

"The Chinese model of global corporatism is superior to the nation-state model, and the transition to the Chinese crony corporate model is inevitable."

The Great Reset would replace the nation-state economic model with Chinese Crony Capitalism.

Marcus Stanley, in his article, "Did Janet Yellen just signal a new world economic order?" [Responsible Statecraft, April 28, 2022.].

"The reality is that Chinese economic integration has already happened. China is now the primary trading partner for manufactured goods of almost two-thirds of the world's 195 nations, including many of the largest and most dynamic economies."

Anne-Marie Slaughter also notes that in addition to Chinese dominance in manufacturing, that the transnational governance networks are already functioning. [Anne-Marie Slaughter The Real New World Order, Foreign Affairs, 1997.].

She writes,

"These courts, regulatory agencies, executives, and legislatures are then networking with their counterparts abroad, creating a new, transgovernmental order… Bankers, lawyers, activists, and criminals…may hold the answer to many of the most pressing international challenges of the 21st century."

The transgovernmental corporatism advocated by the WEF places the police power of the state, in the hands of unelected and unaccountable corporate and banking elites, with no legitimate authority derived from the consent of the governed.

In other words, the new world order creates an all-powerful Leviathan, with awesome terrible powers to compel obedience to the new corporate rulers.

In her article, "Corporatism Goes Global," Marina Ottaway describes the first call for the Great Rest in 1999. [Carnegie Endowment For International Peace, September 2001.].

She writes,

"In January 1999, speaking at the World Economic Forum in Davos, Switzerland, United Nations Secretary-General Kofi Annan proposed a "global compact" between the UN, business, and civil society to tackle the crucial and contentious issues of environmental protection and human and workers' rights. The tripartite model-an international organization, civil society (NGOs and labor organizations) and business-was evident in this initiative as well."

She notes the similarity between the Swedish socialist corporatist model and the model proposed by Kofi Annan,

"Big business, big labor organizations, and international organizations: the global compact was an attempt to recreate at the global level the corporatist tripartite arrangements including government, business and labor unions familiar to many European and Latin American countries."

She continues to explain what global corporatism would look like,

"Corporatism is a system that gives a variety of functional interest groups-most prominently business organizations and labor unions-direct representation in the political system, defusing conflict among them and creating instead broad consensus on policies. Corporatism is thus an answer-not necessarily a good one-to the question of democratic participation."

In global corporatism, corporations replace the current functions of elected representatives. This arrangement of power is a modification and variation of the Italian corporate fascism of Mussolini, whose government directed the big corporations how to function on behalf of state interests.

In the new version of global corporate fascism, the corporations direct the agencies of the Leviathan how they can work together to meet the goals of the corporations.

To answer Schwab's question, above, on who or what "selects the civil society organizations" that are to rule the world, the corporations, acting as government, pick and select the political identity interest groups deserving of representation in the negotiated benefits of global trade, as well as selecting the organizations and individuals who speak for the interest groups.

Corporatism, in its global fascist, authoritarian form resets the nation-state system of representation to one of total corporate political control, with the Leviathan government as the gatekeeper that selects a few carefully chosen, compliant organizations to the negotiation table.

The WEF 2019 document, entitled, "Global Technology Governance: A Multi-stakeholder Approach," explains,

"[The nation-state model] of governance are, on the whole, failing to deliver what is needed in terms of minimizing risks and costs, while maximizing opportunities and benefits. [The] global technology governance goal is to highlight the common priorities, barriers, and roles of stakeholders in unlocking the benefits of emerging technologies while managing their negative impacts."

Gladden Pappin notes that a form the global corporatist negotiation model already functions in the form of the American lobbyist special interest political system.

The American lobbying groups of labor and business is much like the Swedish model of negotiation. [Gladden Pappin, Corporatism for the Twenty-First Century, American Affairs Journal, 2020.].

Pappin advocates for a more formal institutional global corporatism, which he claims, would be an improvement over the secret negotiations of lobbyists and agents of government in the United States.

In the more formal institutional American corporatism, he writes,

"The government grants a "representational monopoly" to each [special interest group] (such as through a system of licensing), and in exchange, [for a seat at the negotiating table], the [special interest groups] must follow certain government-prescribed rules of operation and allow government input on policy…The point of a corporatist model is to create unitary organizations for stakeholders in a particular political system…no matter how profitable industries seek to [lobby] spend on political influence, every economic sector and major social interest has a direct say in decision-making on matters that affect them…Even [wealthy] families are also interest groups of a sort."

The vulnerability of corporate globalism is in its static institutional straight-jacket that locks the existing set of special interests into a permanent political arrangement.

Once the major special identity groups are granted special representational status at the negotiating table, neither citizen participatory democracy, nor newly created special interests have influence in the system to gain future representation.

In their article, Corporatism and the Ghost of the Third Way Randall Morck and Bernard Yeung describe how the corporatism negotiating model becomes a permanent defense of the status quo arrangement of political power. [SSRN 2010.].

They write,

"Corporatism protects existing jobs, businesses, and industries; sheltering all from innovation and instability. Thus, workers need not invest in the human capital accumulation that liberal economies demand for continued high employment, and that econometric evidence indicates is a first order factor in economic growth (Glaeser et al. 2004)…Likewise, cartelized corporatist industries are free from competition to innovate. Thus, corporatism's organization of the economy through cooperation between established businesses, organized labor, and the state excludes the innovative entrants that appear most important in fueling economic growth"

The defect in the corporatist negotiating model is the inability for the system to innovate, and technological innovation is the lynchpin of future economic growth.

In other words, on a global scale, corporatism leads the world economy to a new lower level of economic growth at a new Nash equilibrium, from which it cannot escape, because there is no radical technological innovation.

As we pointed out above, radical technological innovation threatens the status quo arrangement of political power. The main logic of the global corporatist negotiation model is to maintain the status quo arrangement of power by eliminating the threat of radical innovation from new entrepreneurial ventures.

The political stability of the crony capitalist version of the corporatist model depends on politically-connected special interests obtaining a flow of unearned benefits from the system, simply because they have a seat at the negotiating table.

There is no philosophical or ideological incompatibility between global corporations and Marxist-communist political agents in defending the status quo. [Laurie Thomas Vass, BLM Marxism and the Emerging Alliance With Global Corporate Crony Capitalism. Clpnewsnetwork, July 2020.].

We write,

"The BLM alliance with crony capitalism is best understood as the capitalist class co-opting BLM with the tool of racism, in order to perpetuate global capitalism…We argue that the recent crony corporate capitalist endorsements of the use of the term "systemic racism" enables the capitalist class to reproduce itself by continually pointing out to BLM that their conditions of oppression are caused by racism, not global crony capitalism.,,To paraphrase Richard D. Wolff, in his Salon article, ["How racism became the essential tool for maintaining a capitalist order"] the capitalist class pits Blacks against Whites to act as a shock absorber for the lack of jobs and choice provided under the older form of monopoly capitalism."

Todd Zywicki, in his article, Rent-Seeking, Crony Capitalism, and the Crony Constitution, explains the connection between global rent-seeking in the global corporatist negotiating model and the promotion of world-wide Marxism, [Supreme Court Economic Review, 2015.].

"The left has come to appreciate that their interests are served through crony capitalism and, equally important, large corporations have come to see that their interests are naturally aligned with the crony capitalist system. Disruptive [radical innovation] entrepreneurial capitalism is the real enemy of today's corporate behemoths, as shown by the earlier story of the transition of Microsoft and other technology firms entrepreneurial to crony capitalist business practices. Corporations, labor unions, politicians, and leftist interest groups have all come to see a natural alignment in crony capitalism and against entrepreneurial capitalism."

In addition to the first defect of the new world order's commitment to the corporatist negotiation model of status quo arrangement of political power, the more serious long-term flaw is the mistaken assumption that the Chinese communist crony corporatism is a superior economic model to the state-sovereign economic growth model.

Leonardo Dinic speculates that the new world order will be led by a Chinese-Russian coalition, after the Ukraine war ends. [Leonardo Dinic, Will China and Russia Lead the 'New World Order?, China/US Focus, May 2022.].

Dinic writes,

"The term New World Order has been used to describe turbulent moments when certain politicians anticipate such significant change in the geopolitical arena that conflict could inevitably give birth to a new, reorganized international system…

China and Russia [see] the opportunity to create a new version of a 'new world order,' which could rely and rest on foundations of multipolarity and a fundamental opposition to liberal democracy and the western financial system, which has become more weaponized via the U.S. dollar reserve system, trade wars, and sanctions… China [is] irreversibly becoming the leader of the world economy."

Robert Muggah, writing a summary of the WEF Forum in January 2018, notes that,

"Chinese leaders proposed a new global economic system built around Beijing…The world's global and national institutions are increasingly incapable of managing stresses to the system. Democracies, it turns out, lack the incentive systems to address higher-order and longer-term imperatives… We are fixated to the forward march of democracies and the underlying principles on which they are based, yet we must learn to compromise and accommodate multiple value systems." [Robert Muggah, 5 Facts You Need to Understand the New Global Order, January 2018.].

Anthony Rowley echoes the urgency of moving away from nation-state democracies to the Chinese communist model.

He writes,

"The borderless world of business is subject to disruption by nationalism, and there is evidence that this is producing friction…a new global economic order that offers the benefits of international economic cooperation but within a framework of [Chinesse] governance that limits the instability and inequality that globalisation has brought. [Anthony Rowley, World Needs a Better Form of Economic Globalisation to Avoid Another Crisis, South China Morning Post, May 2022.].

The advocacy of the Chinese communist political model are written from the perspective that U. S. global corporations are opposed to China's dominance. However, we argue that the Chinese model of communist crony capitalism is not inconsistent with the U. S. model of crony corporate capitalism.

The flaw in the logic of the Chinese model is that it is incapable of generating economic growth because it is incapable of technology innovation, unless it can steal technology from U. S. corporations.

There is no resistance to the dominance of the Chinese communist model because there is no political opposition to the philosophy in the Republican Party, which serves as the voice of American crony corporatism.

The writer, eugyppius, notes in his recent article, "On the Failure of Conservatives to Mount Effective Opposition to the Most Insane Policies Ever Visited Upon Mankind: Remarks inspired by Manfred Kleine-Hartlage's 'Invective against Conservatives', [AWIP website, May 2022.]. writes,

"Conservatives repeatedly embrace the principles of their opponents, while rejecting nationalists and traditionalists to their right as filthy populists, in chorus with leftist activists themselves… The US Republican Party and also many nominally right-wing mouthpieces, so the line goes, have been co-opted either by the leftist establishment or by related special interests, and function merely as conduits to direct ideological energies towards ineffective or counter-productive ends."

In other words, U. S. crony capitalists have co-opted both the Marxist Democrat Party and the Republican Party, to the end that there is no political opposition in the two party American political system to the new world order implementation of the Chinese communist crony capitalist economic model.

We agree with Todd Zywicki's analysis of American corporatism, as a rent-seeking political model, but disagree with his conclusion about the virtue of the U. S. Constitution as a remedy to corporatism, or as resistance to the new world order.

Zywicki writes,

"In the United States, the term "crony capitalism" refers to a political-economic system that resembles traditional political "corporatism." As used here, it describes a system in which government, big business, and powerful interest groups (especially labor unions) work together to further their joint interests… government creates rents and then distributes them to itself and favored interests in an economy in which rent-seeking is taken as an ordinary incidence of business operations and a legal and socially legitimized way in which wealth can be acquired and maintained by private industry through the use of political influence rather than through market success." [Supreme Court Economic Review, 2015.].

Zywicki explains the co-option of agents of government by the corporate rent-seeking, and we add and modify his analysis to extend to the co-option of BLM Marxist activists in the Democrat Party.

He writes,

"Government is implicitly seen as a partner to the [rent-seeking] transaction in that politicians likewise see private industry as a means for advancing their political interests as well the government—it will protect certain politically-connected firms
from the rigors of competition, thereby guaranteeing those firms and industries a certain flow of revenues. In (implicit) exchange for this guaranteed flow of revenues, the firm promises to share some of that surplus with politically-favored groups, such as labor unions or favored interest groups (such as environmental groups), and with the politicians themselves through campaign contributions and other means of support."

The WEF seeks to extend this rent-seeking corporatist model to the world, in its promotion of the new world order.

In the new world order, corporations replace elected representatives in nation-state democracies, and the so-called "one-world global government" is a Leviathan, disconnected from the consent of the governed.

Zywicki gets the story about the U. S. Constitution wrong.

He claims the standard naively optimistic recitation that Madison's constitution was created to protect against special interest manipulation of government.

He writes,

"The purpose of the Constitution was to try to tame the influence of rent-seekers by using various structural institutions such as separation of powers and federalism to fragment power and thereby to reduce the ability of special-interest factions to commandeer the power of the government for their advantage…The central purpose of the federal Constitution, therefore, was twofold: first, to protect and promote individual liberty and second, to frustrate the efforts by special interest factions to capture the government for their narrow benefit. Put differently, the goal of the Framers was to avoid institutionalized rent-seeking."

We argue, instead, that the purposes of Madison's rules were to eliminate the influence of common citizens in creation of government policies, create a banking and monetary system for wealthy elites to engage in plunder, and protect the institution of slavery. [Laurie Thomas Vass, America's Final Revolution: Reconstructing Jefferson's American Dream of An Entrepreneurial Capitalist Society, The Great American Business & Economics Press. 2022. GABBYPress.com].

We agree with Jefferson that "all legitimate authority is derived from the consent of the governed," and that Madison's constitution is not a useful weapon to defeat the new world order because Madison failed to state that the purpose of his constitution was to protect individual liberty from a centralized tyranny.

The common citizens, in Madison's constitution were left defenseless to protect their liberties, and even Madison's one thin shred of citizen authority on voting for who was to represent them, was eliminated in the election of November 2020.

The term the proponents of the new world order use to describe their superior economic and political model is "stakeholder capitalism." which functions much like the model of special interest negotiation between labor unions and large corporations, in Sweden, prior to 1980.

The proponents of the new world order are fond of calling stakeholder capitalism "Our Democracy," because all relevant stakeholders, as collectivist groups, would gain a seat at the negotiating table.

In their ideology, representative democracy is flawed because collectivist identity groups are marginalized by the voting process. Under corporatism, corporate elites would select which groups were privileged to sit at the table to rule the world.

We have argued that the new world order ideology is vulnerable to attack from nation-state proponents of individualism and entrepreneurial capitalism, both of which cannot be controlled by a new world elite fascist regime.

We agree with Juan Vicente, in his article, "The Reaction Against Individualism and the Remote Origins of Corporatism," that the conflict between the ideology of corporate communism and individualism is irreconcilable. [Capitalism and Society 2018, Reprinted in SSRN.].

Vicente writes,

"Corporatism embodies a system of interest representation in which the constituent units are organized into a limited number of compulsory, noncompeting, hierarchically ordered, and functionally differentiated bodies, existing at the behest or pleasure of the state…"

Vicente explains the vulnerability of new world order corporatism as resistance to new ideas and a commitment to maintain the status quo distribution of economic and political power.

He writes,

"In its attack on individualism and pluralism, [new world order] corporatism is the heir of a long tradition of political thought that rejects "reason" as the source of political legitimacy…Under this model, new ideas and products are not easily accepted unless they arise from inside state regulation. For example, a corporatist state may promote scientific research, especially with public and not private funding; however, the translation of the results of the research into new products must be authorized by the state. Recognized companies can innovate, but only according to the conditions established in the collective bargaining among the state, businesses (through their natural representatives—that is organizations or corporations), and the workers (through their trade unions)."

Vicente's description fits the political and economic failure of Swedish crony socialist corporatism, and the continued existence of Chinese crony corporate communism.

In both Swedish crony corporate socialism, and Chinese crony corporate communism, Vicente writes,

"The social organism [collectivist state] is superior to the individual; the common good is superior to the individual good. The state, [the corporate state] as an expression of the common good, is superior to the will of the individual, and individualism should be opposed, not promoted, since it is the enemy of the common good. [Corporatists] despise uncontrolled innovation and creativity of the dynamic segments of society as an attack on the natural equilibrium [political status quo]. The fate of these corporatist-based governments has been a long and sad story that could be called "a study in failure," since that is the consequence of the political and economic stagnation caused by corporatism."

The flaw in the WEF model of global corporatism is that the economic model is incapable of generating global economic growth because it is incapable of generating radical technological innovation.

And, the benefits of whatever small amount of economic growth happens to be generated is tightly controlled the few corporate and financial elites who manage and administer the model.

Beyond the flaw of corporate fascism over individual free will, the entire globalist political system is founded upon brutal police power of the state to compel obedience.

The only viable alternative to the WEF corporatist fascism is a system called "entrepreneurial capitalism." [Laurie Thomas Vass, America's Final Revolution: Reconstructing Jefferson's American Dream of An Entrepreneurial Capitalist Society,The Great American Business & Economics Press. 2022. GABBYPress.com].

We agree with the conclusion of Baumol, et al,.

They write,

"The continuing emergence and growth of innovative companies -- or what we label "entrepreneurial capitalism" -- stands in stark contrast to the dominance of large firms and unions in the United States in the decades immediately after the end of World War II, and also to the continuing dominance of large firms in Western Europe and Japan. Looking ahead, then, if the United States wishes to continue enjoying rapid growth, it must find a way both to launch and promote the growth of innovative entrepreneurial enterprises and to ensure that the successful entrepreneurs [can] grow their businesses into large firms." [William J. Baumol, Robert E. Litan, Carl J Schramm, Sustaining Entrepreneurial Capitalism, Capitalism and Society, 2007. Reprinted SSRN 2013.].

The entrepreneurial capitalist economic model is decentralized to 50 states, located in 300 metro regions, where radical innovation takes place.

The secret to the successful implementation of entrepreneurial capitalism requires the existing 50 state governments to re-assume their political sovereignty of independent nation-states, first granted to them by King George, when he surrendered British sovereignty to the patriots in 1783.

King George stated,

"In the Name of the Most Holy and Undivided Trinity" Britain acknowledges the United States (New Hampshire, Massachusetts Bay, Rhode Island and Providence Plantations, Connecticut, New York, New Jersey, Pennsylvania, Delaware, Maryland, Virginia, North Carolina, South Carolina, and Georgia to be free, sovereign, and independent states."

The free, sovereign and independent states must never relinquish the sovereignty of the citizens to the corporatist fascist elites of the WEF, who seek to rule the world.

Rather, the mission of the state governments is to do what Jefferson directed them to do, when he stated that,

"We hold these truths to be self-evident, that all men are created equal, that they are endowed by their Creator with certain unalienable Rights, that among these are Life, Liberty and the pursuit of Happiness.--That to secure these rights, Governments are instituted among Men, ***deriving their just powers from the consent of the governed***, --That whenever any Form of Government becomes destructive of these ends, it is the Right of the People to alter or to abolish it, and to institute new Government…"

Legitimate authority to govern is not derived from the stakeholder corporatist model, it is derived from individual citizens, in a free, democratic republic that promotes the ideology that every citizen has the right to be an entrepreneurial capitalist.

Bibliography

Abramovitz, M., and David, P., "Convergence and Deferred Catch-Up: Productivity and the Waning American Exceptionalism," in R. Landau, T. Taylor, G. Wright [Eds.], The Mosaic of Economic Growth, Stanford University Press. 1996.

Adams, R., Paths of Fire: An Anthropologists Inquiry Into Western Technology, Princeton University Press. 1996.

Aligicia, Paul, and Tarko, Vlad, "Crony Capitalism: Rent Seeking, Institutions and Ideology," Kyklos, May 2014.

Autor, David H., Dorn, David, Hanson, Gordon H., "The China Syndrome: Local Labor Market Effects of Import Competition in the United States," American Economic Review, October 2013.

Bell, M., and Pavitt, K., cited in Globalization, Information Technology and Development, J. James, MacMillan Press. 1999.

Bertuglia, C., et al., "An Interpretive Survey of Innovative Behavior and Diffusion," in C. Bertuglia, S. Lombardo, P. Nijkamp, [Eds.], Innovative Behavior In Space and Time, Springer. 1997.

Best, M,, The New Competition: Institutions of Industrial Restructuring, Harvard University Press. 1990.

Blaug, M., Economic History and the History of Economics, New York University Press. 1986.

Bohman, James, "Critical Theory, Republicanism, and the Priority of Injustice: Transnational Republicanism as a Nonideal Theory," Journal of Social Philosophy, 2012.

Boland, R., and Tenkasi, R., "Perspective Making and Perspective Taking In Communities of Knowing," in G. DeSanctis and J. Fulk [Eds.], Shaping Organizational Form: Communication, Connection and Community, Sage Public. 1996.

Borjas, George, Immigration Economics, Harvard University Press, 2014.

Breitbart News, "Eve of Destruction: Klaus Schwab Pledges the World Can Find Salvation at Davos 2022, May 19, 2022.

Bruno, A., and T. Tyebjee, "The Environment For Entrepreneurship," in C. Kent, D. Sexton, and K. Vesper, The Encyclopedia of Entrepreneurship, Prentice-Hall, Inc. 1982.

Bryce, David and Winter, Sidney, A General Inter-Industry Relatedness Index, CES Working Paper 06-31, 2006.

Carlsson, B., "Technological Systems and Economic Development Potential: Four Swedish Case Studies," in Y. Shionoya, and M. Perlman, Innovation in Technology, Industries and Institutions: Studies In Schumpeterian Perspectives, University of Michigan Press. 1994.

Christensen, Clayton, Efosa Ojomo, Gabrielle Gay, Philip Auerswald, How Market-Creating Innovation Drives

Economic Growth and Development, Innovations / Blockchain for Global Development, 2019.

Christensen, Clayton M., The Innovator's Dilemma: When New Technologies Cause Great Firms to Fail, Harvard Business Press, 2016.

Christensen, Clayton, Seeing What's Next: Using Theories of Innovation to Predict Industry Change, Harvard Business Press, 2004.

Christensen, Clayton M., et al., The Third Answer: How Market-Creating Innovations Drives Economic Growth and Development, Innovations, 2018.

Coombs, R., P. Saviotti, and V. Walsh, Economics and Technological Change, Rowman and Littlefield. 1987.

Decker, Ryan A., Haltiwanger, John, Jarmin, Ron S., Miranda, Javier, "Declining Dynamism, Allocative Efficiency, and the Productivity Slowdown," American Economic Review, May 2017.

Dinic, Leonardo, "Will China and Russia Lead the 'New World Order?", China/US Focus, May 2022.

Duchin, F., "Structural Economics: Measuring Change In Technology, Lifestyles and the Environment," Island Press. 1998.

Ellis, Curtis, "China's Post-Virus Plan to Destroy America's Economy," Prosperous America, 2020.

Evans, P., and T. Wurster, Blown to Bits: How The New Economics of Information Transforms Strategy, Harvard University Press. 2000.

Feser, E. J. and Sweeney, S. H., Industrial Complexes Revisited: A Test of For Coincident Economic and Spatial Clustering, Working Paper, Department of City and Regional Planning, University of North Carolina, 1997.

Gingrich, Newt. Quoted in The Hill, October 25, 2019.

Graceffo, Antonio, "China's National Champions: State Support Makes Chinese Companies Dominant," Foreign Policy Journal, May 15, 2017.

Hanusch, H., Evolutionary Economics: Applications of Schumpeter's Ideas, Cambridge: Cambridge University Press. 1988.

Heertje, A., "Schumpeter and Technical Change," in Hanusch, H.[Ed.], Evolutionary Economics: Applications of Schumpeter's Ideas, Cambridge University Press. 1988.

Henrekson, Magnus, Jakobsson, Ulf, "Where Schumpeter was Nearly Right: The Swedish Model and Capitalism, Socialism and Democracy, Journal of Evolutionary Economics, 2001. Reprinted in SSRN. 2007.

Hicks, J. R., Value and Capital, Clarendon Press. 1939.

Houseman, Susan, Understanding the Decline of U.S. Manufacturing Employment, Upjohn Institute for Employment Research, 2018.

Jacobs, J., Cities and the Wealth of Nations: Principles of Economic Life, Random House. 1984.

Jaffe. A., "Technological Opportunity and Spillovers of R & D: Evidence From Firm's Patents, Profits, and Market Value," American Economic Review, 1986.

Kuhn, Thomas, The Structure of Scientific Revolutions, University of Chicago Press, 1962.

Kuznets, S., Secular Movements In Production and Prices, Houghton, Mifflin. 1930.

Kuznets, Simon, Modern Economic Growth: Findings and Reflections, 1971.

Leontief, W., "Input-Output Data Base For Analysis of Technological Change," Economic Systems Research, 1989.

Lynn, Leonard, and Salzman, Hal,"Collaborative Advantage," Issues In Science and Technology, Winter 2006.

Malerba, F., and L. Orsenigo, "Schumpeterian Patterns of Innovation," in D. Archibugi and J. Michie [Eds.], Technology, Globalization and Economic Performance, Cambridge University Press. 1997.

Malloch, Theodore Roosevelt, "Exposing the Roots of Globalism," American Greatness, April, 2020.

Minsky, H., "Schumpeter: Finance and Evolution," in A. Heertje and M. Perlman [Eds.], Evolving Technology and

Market Structure: Studies in Schumpeterian Economics, University of Michigan Press. 1990.

Mokyr, J., The Lever of Riches: Technological Creativity and Economic Progress, Oxford University Press. 1990.

Morck, Randall, and Yeung, Bernard, "Corporatism and the Ghost of the Third Way," SSRN 2010.

Moretti, Enrico, "Local Multipliers," American Economic Review: Papers & Proceedings, 2010.

Morroni, M., Production Processes and Technical Change, Cambridge University Press. 1992.

Mowery, D., Paths of Innovation: Technical Change in the 20th Century, Cambridge University Press. 1998.

Muggah, Robert, "5 Facts You Need to Understand the New Global Order," January 2018.

Ottaway, Marina, "Corporatism Goes Global," Carnegie Endowment For International Peace, September 2001.

Pappin, Gladden, "Corporatism for the Twenty-First Century," American Affairs Journal, 2020.

Pasinetti, L., Structural Change and Economic Growth: A Theoretical Essay on The Dynamics of the Wealth of Nations, Cambridge University Press. 1981.

Phelps, Edmund, Refounding Capitalism, Capitalism and Society, 2009. Reprinted in SSRN.

Porat, Marc Uri, The Information Economy: Definition and Measurement, U. S. Department of Commerce, O. T. Special Publication 77-12[1]. 1977.

Rogers, E., "Diffusions of Innovations," cited in R. Goel [Ed.], Economic Models of Technological Change: Theory and Application, Quorum Books. 1999.

Rogers, E., Diffusion of Innovation, Fourth Edition, The Free Press. 1995.

Rostow, W. W., The Process of Economic Growth, Norton & Co., 1962.

Rowley, Anthony, "World Needs a Better Form of Economic Globalisation to Avoid Another Crisis," South China Morning Post, May 2022.

Saviotti, P., Technological Evolution, Variety and the Economy, Edward-Elgar. 1996.

Schumpeter, J. A. The Theory of Economic Development. Harvard University Press. 1934. First published in German in 1911.

Schumpeter, J. A., Capitalism, Socialism and Democracy. George Allen & Unwin. 1942.

Schwab, Klaus, and Smadjav, Claude, "Power and Policy: The New Economic World Order, Harvard Business Review, 1994.

Slaughter, Anne-Marie, "The Real New World Order," Foreign Affairs, 1997.

Stanley, Marcus, "Did Janet Yellen just signal a new world economic order?" Responsible Statecraft, April 28, 2022.

Stuttaford, Andrew, "The Great Reset: If Only It Were Just a Conspiracy, National Review," November, 2020.

Temin, P., "Entrepreneurs and Managers," in P. Higonnet, D. Landes, and H. Rosovsky, [Eds.], Favorites of Fortune, Harvard University Press. 1991.

Vass, Laurie Thomas, "Searching for Signs of Technological Innovation in the Ruins of the American Economy," August 4, 2008. Available at SSRN.

Vass, Laurie Thomas, "Who Is It In America That Is Responsible For Implementing the Trade Agreements With China?" CLP News Network, March 2022.

Vass, Laurie Thomas, "Using Feser's Input-Output Model of Technological Affinities To Target Innovation Investments To Regional Industrial Value Chains," SSRN, 2008.

Vass, Laurie Thomas, "BLM Marxism and the Emerging Alliance With Global Corporate Crony Capitalism. Clpnewsnetwork, July 2020.

Vass, Laurie Thomas, America's Final Revolution: Reconstructing Jefferson's American Dream of An Entrepreneurial Capitalist Society, The Great American Business & Economics Press. 2022.

Vicente, Juan, "The Reaction Against Individualism and the Remote Origins of Corporatism," Capitalism and Society, 2018. Reprinted in SSRN.

Wolff, E., "Spillovers, Linkages and Technical Change," Economic Systems Research, 1997.

Wolff, Richard D., "How racism became the essential tool for maintaining a capitalist order,"Salon, June 26, 2020.

Worstall, Tim, "Larry Summers And The Productivity Puzzle," Forbes, Feb 21, 2015.

Yasar, Ayse Gizem, "Re-examining Schumpeter's Legacy: Creative Destruction as Competition," Innovation and Capitalism, reprinted in SSRN 2021.

Zywicki, Todd J., "Rent-Seeking, Crony Capitalism, and the Crony Constitution," Supreme Court Economic Review, Forthcoming; George Mason Legal Studies Research Paper No. LS 15-08; George Mason Law & Economics Research Paper No. 15-26. August 26, 2015. Available at SSRN).

www.ingramcontent.com/pod-product-compliance
Lightning Source LLC
LaVergne TN
LVHW051950060526
838201LV00059B/3592